THE
BIG SLAM

BY BILL CORBETT

★

★

DRAMATISTS
PLAY SERVICE
INC.

THE BIG SLAM
Copyright © 1999, Bill Corbett

All Rights Reserved

SPECIAL NOTE

CHARACTERS

RUSSELL BOAM — an entrepreneur
STEPHANIE ROMMEL — an attorney
ORRIN HOOVER — an historian/temp
GAIL MYSZLWESKI — a UPS driver/artist

All four are somewhere in their mid-twenties — mid-thirties

SETTING

New York City. Various locations: a bar, an apartment, an office, a rooftop.

NOTES

Sets should be as simple. Ideally, no air-time at all between scenes: Orrin's direct talks to the audience should be used to cover any scene changes. These are all indicated by the word "out," in parentheses. Where these monologues aren't there to do that, the characters can travel from one scene to the next, already engaged in the dialogue.

THE BIG SLAM was produced by A Contemporary Theatre (Gordon Edelstein, Artistic Director; Susan Baird Trapnell, Managing Director) in Seattle, Washington, on October 21, 1997. It was directed by Howard Shalwitz; the assistant director was Elizabeth Crane; the set design was by Jeff Frkonja; the costume design was by David Zinn; the lighting design was by Rick Paulsen; the sound design was by David Pascal; and the stage manager was Jeffrey K. Hanson. The cast was as follows:

RUSSELL..Mark Deklin Schwötzer
ORRIN ....Willie Weir
STEPHANIE ....Shelley Reynolds
GAIL...Julie Gustafson

THE BIG SLAM was produced by Woolly Mammoth Theatre Company (Howard Shalwitz, Artistic Director; Imani Drayton-Hill, Managing Director) in Washington, D.C., in October, 1998. It was directed by Casey Stangl; the set design was by Tony Cisek; the costume design was by Brooke Edwards; the lighting design was by Dan Covey; the sound design was by Daniel Schrader; the production manager was Rick Fiori; and the stage manager was Cheryl Repeta. The cast was as follows:

RUSSELL ....Christopher Lane
ORRIN...John Kirkman
STEPHANIE ....Carol Monda
GAIL ....Rhea Seehorn

THE BIG SLAM was commissioned and originally produced by Eye of the Storm (Casey Stangl, Artistic Director; John Spokes, Managing Director) in Minneapolis, Minnesota, on October 20, 1995. It was directed by Casey Stangl; the set design was by Steve Griffith; the costume design was by Patsy Monson; the lighting design was by Barry Browning; the sound design was by Michael Croswell; the dramaturgs were Chad Sylvain and Elissa Adams; and the stage manager was Lucinda C.S. Obenhaus. The cast was as follows:

RUSSELL ....Jeff Tatum
ORRIN ....Peter Breitmayer
STEPHANIE ....Mo Collins
GAIL ....Sandy Thomas

THE BIG SLAM

ACT ONE

Spot on Orrin. He talks directly to the audience.

ORRIN. *(Out.)* I've always been shy. That's indisputable. But it became what one might call pathological when I was around Russell. He seemed to have a magnetism to people. I evaporated next to him. For a while, in my heart, I thought, "Well, I'm probably smarter, even if he is much better-looking, more charming, more confident, more articulate, and all that." But one day I realized: "No, he's smarter too." That was disturbing. *(Music. Lights up on Russell, at a table in a bar, deep in concentration. Orrin joins him.)*

RUSSELL. What, what, what? What could it be? What is it?

ORRIN. Yeah, what is it?

RUSSELL. What's the thing? The new take?

ORRIN. The thing, right.

RUSSELL. The new angle ...

ORRIN. The new thing ... *(Corrects himself.)* I mean, angle ...

RUSSELL. Great ideas come unbidden, you just have to make a little clearance ...

ORRIN. Right.

RUSSELL. OK, let me think laterally, here, just a second ...

ORRIN. Laterally? That's new.

RUSSELL. The unexpected thing ... That which is so new it's always been there, since ancient days ... Obvious without yet being seized upon ...

ORRIN. I'm trying to think of it too ...

RUSSELL. I read about this one paradigm master ... Problem was, everyone in this big office building is complaining the elevators are taking too long. Owners of the building hire this guy, they say: "Should we make them go faster? That would really cost, but ... These complainants, they're making our lives miserable ..." Guy looks over the situation two seconds, his mind starts buzzing and humming, click click click, then — ingenious! — he goes: "Nahhh. Save your money!" And he tells them to install these big mirrors at the lobby elevator banks so people can look at themselves, get involved in a momentary narcissism so they don't feel the horrible weight of time passing through their lives.

ORRIN. Boy.

RUSSELL. *Quite* lateral, I'd say.

ORRIN. Yeah.

RUSSELL. Click click click ... Getting strong feelings! Absolutely crystalline feelings, that the next step is tonight.

ORRIN. Tonight? I was going to go home soon.

RUSSELL. Knock and the door shall open ...

ORRIN. I have a pretty interesting book going.

RUSSELL. Laterally ... *lateral* ... *(Enter Stephanie, with a drink, dressed tastefully sexy. She sits nearby.)*

ORRIN. It's about the Visigoths. Did you know that when they invaded the Holy Roman Empire, that the Romans — ?

RUSSELL. Hey, take a look at her!

ORRIN. Wow.

RUSSELL. Click click click ... Yeah! This is it.

ORRIN. What is?

RUSSELL. *She* is.

ORRIN. Really?

RUSSELL. Hey! Hey, Miss!

ORRIN. Russell, what are you doing?

RUSSELL. Following the lead, bud. The impulse. Hey Miss! Miss? *(Stephanie turns slowly.)*

STEPHANIE. Did your puppy run away?

RUSSELL. I'm sorry?

STEPHANIE. I thought perhaps you were calling a lost dog.

RUSSELL. Sorry. Tragically uncool.

STEPHANIE. Don't shout across the room at me. You want to talk? Be civilized. Approach me.

RUSSELL. "Approach." That's great!

STEPHANIE. Yes. Humbly.

RUSSELL. Approaching. With tremendous humility.

ORRIN. *(Whispers.)* Um, Russell? Should I come too?

RUSSELL. *(Whispers.)* For now. — Hello. May we sit?

STEPHANIE. If you feel compelled. *(Russell sits in the only free seat. Orrin hovers.)*

RUSSELL. Hi. Say Orrin, would you be so kind as to get us a round of mineral waters?

ORRIN. *(Whispers.)* Domestic mineral waters? Because I think that's all we can afford, at this point —

RUSSELL. Fine. Some of those raspberry essence flavored ones, maybe.

ORRIN. You want anything, Miss?

STEPHANIE. I want *everything.*

ORRIN. Oh. So then…?

STEPHANIE. Nothing at the moment, though.

ORRIN. Oh. *(Exits.)*

STEPHANIE. Mineral waters? You gentlemen walking the twelve steps?

RUSSELL. *(Big smile.)* No, ma'am.

STEPHANIE. I — obviously — am not. Overdid it tonight.

RUSSELL. No judgement from me. It's a complete waste of energy to judge.

STEPHANIE. Deep.

RUSSELL. *(Laughs.)* I try. Though they make it hard to delve below the surface in this workaday world.

STEPHANIE. And what specific world would that be?

RUSSELL. Currently doing this abysmal temp job.

STEPHANIE. Ahhh. A "job."

RUSSELL. Yes.

STEPHANIE. Jobs are … deadly.

RUSSELL. Yes! A good premise to start from.

STEPHANIE. Jobs *suck.*

RUSSELL. Yes! They leave me too empty inside to do what I really want.

STEPHANIE. And what is that?

RUSSELL. Have an impact. Be fulfilled.

STEPHANIE. Me too …

RUSSELL. Find a new way to —

STEPHANIE. Find a new way to ... be.

RUSSELL. Right out of my mouth! Synchronicity.

STEPHANIE. And I need aesthetic pleasure, also, or I'm doomed. That workaday world? Like you said? It makes me wonder if there's any beauty in life. Any patterns which work.

RUSSELL. There are.

STEPHANIE. You know them?

RUSSELL. Learning, ever learning.

STEPHANIE. They have got to be found. I have got to find these fucking patterns.

RUSSELL. I *am* going to find them. I'm absolutely, 100% sure that I'll find them. I'm on a vision quest. I don't care what it takes, or if I have to make a total fool of myself in the search. I'm finding them.

STEPHANIE. You ... mean that?

RUSSELL. Yes, I do. Nothing else matters. I'm finding those patterns.

STEPHANIE. God. If only, if only ...

RUSSELL. You're really attractive.

STEPHANIE. Is that so?

RUSSELL. Yes. *(Pause.)* Well?

STEPHANIE. Well what?

RUSSELL. Reaction to my statement?

STEPHANIE. You've made quite a few. Which one?

RUSSELL. You being attractive.

STEPHANIE. You want me to weep in gratitude? What?

RUSSELL. Just a reaction.

STEPHANIE. A reaction. OK. Let me surprise you deeply.

RUSSELL. Please.

STEPHANIE. You are quite attractive too.

RUSSELL. Wow. Stunned. Very happy.

STEPHANIE. Glad I could help.

RUSSELL. You want to ... be together somewhere?

STEPHANIE. It wouldn't be nice, leaving your friend without a word.

RUSSELL. He'll be fine. He's my best friend! He understands these situations.

STEPHANIE.   Just doesn't seem like the best of ... manners.

RUSSELL.   Not my specialty, maybe. Manners.

STEPHANIE.   They aren't terribly ... functional, are they? *(They laugh.)*

RUSSELL.   But I can be courtly. Very courtly, and very ... chivalrous. I would like to be courtly with you. Tonight.

STEPHANIE.   Would you? *(She runs one finger across his face, softly, exploring its contours. It's a light touch, but sexy.)* All right. Court me. *(Lights down on them. Spot on Orrin.)*

ORRIN.   *(Out.)* They didn't have raspberry. In that couple of minutes where I decided what fruit would be a good alternative, I lost Russell. It wasn't the first time he fell off the map, though it was the longest. As often, it involved love ... or what he called love. And as per usual, he did not return phone calls for a while, then also as per usual, his line was suddenly disconnected; with no forwarding number. Russell and I were graduate students together. Me in history, he in a number of areas, all left abandoned for the next. At a not-very-impressive university. Everyone there agreed that Russell was simply slumming it in some way; biding time until his Big Life Move. At which point it would basically be — in uppercase, this is — "Watch Out World, Here He Comes." Russell did nothing to discourage such speculation. Nevertheless, upon graduation the severe lack of employment opportunities for minor-league academics landed us both squarely in the New York office temp subculture, where our most elementary abilities to read and count were utilized but not exactly ... challenged. And these low-wattage tasks were remunerated in a commensurate way. Which is to say, they paid like shit. These were the seeds of our discontent. I followed his lead because he saw a way out, and I did not. Furthermore, he could lead. He was *willing* to lead. I knew I could not; would not; and never had. *(Lights down on him. Up on Russell and Stephanie, in bed together, in the throes of passion.)*

STEPHANIE.   Come on, come on ...

RUSSELL.   Yes, yes ...

STEPHANIE.   Give me kisses, all over, come on ...

RUSSELL.   Yes, I will ...

STEPHANIE. Keep kissing me!

RUSSELL. Man, this is phenomenal ...

STEPHANIE. It is!

RUSSELL. Usually I'm the one begging for a little extra energy and life, but we're on the same wavelength ...

STEPHANIE. We are! In bed, anyway ...

RUSSELL. But that's what I mean! That says a lot! We both reach down into ourselves, and pull out this natural force ...

STEPHANIE. We do! Like animals!

RUSSELL. Yes! We go right to the primacy of our core beings, and intermingle a kind of —

STEPHANIE. I'm gonna be on top for a while! *(She flips them over.)*

RUSSELL. Whoa! That was great! You are *strong*, woman!

STEPHANIE. That's right! I could kick your ass!

RUSSELL. Feel these legs of yours! All muscle! Like sculpted out of wood!

STEPHANIE. What kind of thing to say is that?

RUSSELL. Pure admiration!

STEPHANIE. You watch what this piece of wood can do to you!

RUSSELL. Pure fascination!

STEPHANIE. I can out-wrestle you!

RUSSELL. Oh, yeah? Feel my stomach, baby! Washboard abdominals!

STEPHANIE. Sshhh ... Stop talking ... Scream at me!

RUSSELL. What?

STEPHANIE. Scream at me, top of your lungs!

RUSSELL. Sure! *(He begins to primal scream.)*

STEPHANIE. A real scream, you wuss! Like this! *(She gives him a real scream. Lights down on them. Up on Orrin, holding a paper bag.)*

ORRIN. *(Out.)* I didn't hear from Russell again until seven months later, when he called at six-thirty A.M. one morning and told me to come over to his new girlfriend's place. Immediately. He said "bring some champagne," but I had a good idea ... *(Lights up on Stephanie's apartment: Russell greets Orrin wearing only his boxer shorts. Orrin carries a paper bag.)*

RUSSELL. Orrin! Buddy! *(He gives Orrin a big bear hug.)* Been too long! Welcome to our humble abode!

ORRIN. Hi, Russell.

RUSSELL. What you have there, the bubbly?

ORRIN. A different kind. *(Russell looks in the bag.)*

RUSSELL. Raspberry sparkling water? What is this, Orrin?

ORRIN. *(Suddenly embarrassed.)* I figured, you know, you had wanted it, you know, and you know, you hadn't gotten it yet, so, you know …

RUSSELL. What the hell are you talking about?

ORRIN. Um, the last time I saw you. In the bar.

RUSSELL. Oh! You were pissed at me! Oh! I see, this is a way of communicating that!

ORRIN. Um, yeah.

RUSSELL. Good stuff! That's a good way of doing it! 'Cause I get the message now. It's sinking in. Already sunk in. Yeah. Pretty slick maneuver, Orrin.

ORRIN. Thanks, Russell.

RUSSELL. Come on in here though, buddy, let's waste no time. *(The UPS Driver, Gail — a perky, pretty young woman — appears at the open door, knocks.)*

GAIL. Umm … Hello?

RUSSELL. Yes?

GAIL. Oh! God, sorry … The door was open …

RUSSELL. I have nothing to hide! Welcome!

GAIL. UPS?

RUSSELL. Welcome, UPS!

GAIL. Package for … Russell Boam?

RUSSELL. All right! Sequence Five, right? You brought us Sequence Five?

GAIL. I … just know that it's a … package, sir.

RUSSELL. It is Sequence Five! Excellent! I could just sit down and eat this stuff!

GAIL. Could you sign for it first please, sir?

RUSSELL. Proudly! *(He signs.)* You've brought us a treasure, um — what's your name?

GAIL. Gail. I'm glad.

RUSSELL. Thanks, Gail! *(She exits.)* Synchronicity, synchronicity ... I'm telling you, buddy, there's a reason why she shows up right now, just as you do! *(He brings the package over, opens it.)* 'Cause look at this ... Look at what we have here, this is why we need a celebratory potable ... Observe! *(He puts the contents — books and tapes — on top of a huge stack already sitting there.)*

ORRIN. What are they?

RUSSELL. The key to fulfillment.

ORRIN. You ... found it? *(Enter Stephanie, in a bathrobe. Groggy; huge cup of coffee in hand.)*

STEPHANIE. We both did. Hi. Remember me?

ORRIN. Umm ... We didn't really meet for too long.

RUSSELL. And he's giving us a little message about that, Stephanie. Look at this! He gave me a bottle of raspberry sparkling shit, to communicate his hurt feelings! Fantastic, huh? This man's got a slyness, untapped by the world to date. A subtlety as yet unappreciated. He's fantastic!

STEPHANIE. I don't get it.

ORRIN. It's a kind of obscure reference by now, I guess.

RUSSELL. Stephanie, this is Orrin Hoover. Orrin, Stephanie Rommel.

ORRIN. Hi.

STEPHANIE. Hi.

RUSSELL. We just got Sequence Five, Steph!

STEPHANIE. Rock and roll! *(She begins hungrily looking through the tapes and books.)*

RUSSELL. You still with the temp job, Orrin?

ORRIN. Yeah. They wondered what happened to you.

RUSSELL. That phase in my life suddenly ended. Tell them that for me, will you, Orrin, when you see them next? Tell it to them just like that: "He said that phase in his life suddenly ended." If they can't fathom that, then they deserve no further word on the matter.

STEPHANIE. This new material looks fabulous!

RUSSELL. But you're still there, you've been steady; good. That click-click-clicks into place just right.

ORRIN. Oh?

RUSSELL. They wondered what happened to me? *This* is what happened to me. This whole thing.

ORRIN.   Books, and tapes?

RUSSELL.   Yes, but Stephanie first. Stephanie is mostly what happened to me. Stephanie has filled my heart. The literature is ancillary to that. Because after she happened to me, the rest? ... the rest what, what is that we call it, honey?

STEPHANIE.   The rest *flowered*.

RUSSELL.   Yeah! Everything else *flowered* after that.

ORRIN.   I see.

RUSSELL.   Stephanie and I have — OK if I speak for us both, honey?

STEPHANIE.   Till I finish my coffee.

RUSSELL.   Stephanie and I have come together in many ways: romantically, sexually; through intense emotional bonding that has involved a dance of joy, catharsis and pain.

STEPHANIE.   Highs, lows, laughter, tears. All about growth, of course.

RUSSELL.   But we have recently had a phenomenal break-through. We have owned up — God, we're giddy about it! ... We —

STEPHANIE.   ... We have owned up to our synthesis in one other important arena:

RUSSELL.   We *are* both extremely fucking ambitious.

STEPHANIE.   We realized it was the premise of our first connection.

RUSSELL.   That time we so rudely ditched out on you. Belated apologies, sincere ones, Orrin.

STEPHANIE.   We *are* sorry. Really.

ORRIN.   That's OK.

RUSSELL.   But it had to happen, bud, to make way for this ... Drumroll, please! *(He gestures to Orrin: "Take it away.")*

ORRIN.   Oh — what?

RUSSELL.   Drumroll! Go ahead. *(Orrin does a halting, arrhythmic drumbeat on the table.)* We're going to start a business together.

ORRIN.   Great.

STEPHANIE.   Not a business, Russell.

RUSSELL.   Did I say "business"? What a submental idiot I am. No. "Business," we agreed, is a tired, dusty, senile word. Very inaccurate for our purposes. We're going to start — Stephanie?

STEPHANIE.   An *enterprise.*

RUSSELL.   Yes! See? An enterprise is more like a path.

ORRIN.   A path.

STEPHANIE.   You can stop drumming now.

ORRIN.   Oh. Sorry. *(He stops.)*

RUSSELL.   Yes, a path! Which few are willing to take. Where the risks are great, but the rewards can be exponentially greater.

STEPHANIE.   Russell's an egghead. He expresses himself with theory.

RUSSELL.   Life is a theory!

STEPHANIE.   I have far less patience for it.

RUSSELL.   Stephanie's a lawyer!

STEPHANIE.   An *attorney.*

RUSSELL.   But she stopped practicing this year. After they threatened to disbar her.

ORRIN.   Wow.

RUSSELL.   It wasn't her fault, though! Like she said, the fucking system just couldn't — !

STEPHANIE.   The reason — what's your name again?

ORRIN.   Orrin.

STEPHANIE.   The reason I was nearly disbarred, Orrin, is this: When we were all young we were told that it's good to be ambitious. So I took it seriously. Became an attorney. A pit bull, wipe-the-floor-with-your-sorry-ass, kind of attorney. And I tried to steal clients. Successfully. Apparently — for a woman — this level of ambition is … distasteful. I accepted the responsibility, but I also said, "Eat me!" Got myself out of that game. That whole world is too confining.

ORRIN.   Sounds … like it.

RUSSELL.   Which brings us to our key to fulfillment! Stephanie and I have leaned back into our ambition, with great relief.

STEPHANIE.   Yes. It's a place of comfort for us. We set the value judgement aside — banished it — and found that sitting in this place of ambition was like being cradled in our mothers' arms. An actual den of nurturing.

RUSSELL. Yes. So we sought and found others who felt the same way. Here! *(Proudly shows him one of the tapes.)*

ORRIN. *(Reads.) Strategies for Power.*

STEPHANIE. A truly amazing home seminar! Books and tapes.

RUSSELL. Remember the lateral thinking I was practicing, Orrin? That was just a little tricycle. This is a Jaguar; this is an Alpha Romeo —

STEPHANIE. We discussed the automotive metaphors, honey?

RUSSELL. Yeah, sorry. Orrin: You wondered, I'm sure, where I'd been sequestered this time? Right here, with Steph, having my consciousness re-shaped.

STEPHANIE. We've been in training.

RUSSELL. This material is mind-boggling, buddy.

ORRIN. Umm. Congratulations?

RUSSELL. Thank you.

STEPHANIE. That's actually an incredibly appropriate response.

ORRIN. Good.

RUSSELL. Now. We want to start an interface with you.

ORRIN. About the business? ... Sorry.

RUSSELL and STEPHANIE. *Enterprise.*

ORRIN. Sorry.

RUSSELL. We want to give you an opportunity to grow in with us.

ORRIN. To grow in — ?

STEPHANIE. In layman's terms: to invest.

RUSSELL. You have some nice savings, as I recall? He lives very frugally, Steph. Budgets everything.

STEPHANIE. How ... exotic.

ORRIN. I've saved pretty well. But — to be honest — I don't think I want to buy a bunch of ... tapes, and stuff.

RUSSELL. "Tapes and stuff"! He's great! Orrin, you don't have to!

STEPHANIE. We have pored over this "stuff," as you call it, Orrin; we've learned, discussed, absorbed; we've undergone osmosis ...

RUSSELL. ... Taken it into our very fucking molecules, gotten the energy way way WAY up, and we're ready to rock! That's

15

what really matters! We said, let's approach our friend Orrin with the barter system. We take you with us on a wonderful journey of the heart and mind, you merely cordon off that ten thousand bucks you currently have for a few months, after which phenomenal returns start rolling in for you.

ORRIN. Ten thousand! That's all my savings, Russell! I've been putting it away since high school. Started it with my paper route ...

RUSSELL. "Paper route"! Orrin, scroll it up to the present tense, buddy!

ORRIN. What?

STEPHANIE. He means you're letting sentimentality rule the day. Pick your feet up out of the mud, he's saying. You're in a mental quagmire.

RUSSELL. Exactly!

ORRIN. Oh. Well — what is it?

RUSSELL. "What is it?" What is what?

ORRIN. The bus — The enterprise. *(Pause. Russell seems genuinely confused.)*

RUSSELL. What are you talking about? "What is it?" What is he talking about? What are you talking about, buddy?

ORRIN. I mean, what are you going to ... sell?

RUSSELL. "Sell?" *(He laughs.)* Oh Orrin, dear old friend, you do not disappoint! Mr. Cart-Before-the-Horse, here!

ORRIN. What?

RUSSELL. We don't *know* yet.

ORRIN. Really?

RUSSELL. Really.

STEPHANIE. Really. And that is the single strongest thing we have going for us right now. We don't know.

RUSSELL. Right, Steph! We say that proudly and unabashedly.

ORRIN. But how can you — ? I mean —

RUSSELL. Good-bye, buddy.

ORRIN. What?

RUSSELL. We'll call you in a few months, take you out to dinner. Buy you some *real* champagne. 'Cause we'll have reason to *really* celebrate, at that point. No hard feelings at all, buddy, just — we don't have time. 'Bye.

STEPHANIE.   Russell, shush.

RUSSELL.   What? I was just —

STEPHANIE.   Ssshh, ssshh, ssshh. Excuse us a second, Orrin. *(She has a more private confab with Russell, though not attempting to hide it from Orrin.)* These are those very moments of Conjunction talked about — at length! — in Sequence Three. The door opens for Bridge-building very, very briefly, and in such moments one has to expand …

RUSSELL.   … Rather than contract, yeah. God, is that what I'm doing?

STEPHANIE.   Most definitely. Contracting like a maniac!

RUSSELL.   Sorry, Stephanie.

STEPHANIE.   Review the material. You're committing a text-book fuck-up here.

RUSSELL.   You're right. Sorry, Steph. Sorry, Orrin.

STEPHANIE.   Now, let's back up a bit. Orrin. Hi. Orrin. We're sorry for our awkwardness in approaching this. We're still on our learning curve. But that aside: We — Russell and I — simply do not want to see this swim away from you. As someone who is soon to be your friend, it would hurt me to see you wallowing in regrets later on. Please, sit down, Orrin. *(Orrin does so.)* Can I get you a sparkling water?

ORRIN.   Yes, thank you. *(Stephanie puts her hand out. Russell grabs a sparkling water from Orrin's bag, opens it, hands it to her. She hands it to Orrin.)* Thank you.

STEPHANIE.   You're most welcome. Now, please relax. *(Stephanie comes around behind him, puts her hands on his shoulders.)* Clear your head. Take a long, deep breath. Another. Another. Now: Forget about the past. That can't help you anymore. Stop looking behind you; it's just shadows.

ORRIN.   I'm not sure —

STEPHANIE.   Ssshh. Clear your head. Close your eyes. *(She massages his temples, speaks softly, slowly, sensually, lulling him.)* There's nothing to gather from where you've been, if you haven't already. Why be an inventory-taker; a bean-counting

17

little clerk, of your own life? When you can be the Creator of that Life?

ORRIN. I don't know —

STEPHANIE. So much of what you've been told has been hurtful to you. Words have been used to wound you, and you need to re-claim those words. They shamed me with words to punish my un-lady-like appetites ... Maybe words have been used to mock you for your gentleness ...

ORRIN. Yes!

STEPHANIE. Shift your vocabulary, and no one can touch you again. Shift your vocabulary, and you shift your thinking, and your past stops looming over you like a ghost. Right now is all that counts. Right now. Think of us, in the room with you, right now. We're about to go on a breathtaking journey. We're all packed; we're excited. And we want you to come with us. Do you — *right now* — want to come with us?

ORRIN. Maybe ... But —

STEPHANIE. *(She breaks away from him.)* You have five seconds, and five seconds only. Then the door slams shut, and we're on our way without you. Five seconds. Are you coming on this trip with us? One ...

RUSSELL. Two ...

STEPHANIE. Three ...

RUSSELL. Four ...

STEPHANIE. F ...

ORRIN. Yes.

STEPHANIE. You don't seem sure.

ORRIN. Yes! *(She grabs the sparkling water out of his hands.)*

STEPHANIE. The conviction isn't reaching your voice, Orrin. Louder!

ORRIN. Yes!

STEPHANIE. Scream it, Orrin! Tell the world!

ORRIN. YES!

STEPHANIE. They can't hear you in Japan! Louder! *(Orrin breaks from the scene. Spot on him.)*

ORRIN. *(Out.)* In one minute I was producing a scream at a decibel level I thought physiologically impossible, for the likes of myself. It was intoxicating! The minute after that I was on the floor, sobbing: begging to give them my ten thousand! They graciously accepted it. A few days later, I came back with a cashier's check. When I found out at that time that I was, in fact, the sole investor — Russell being broke and Stephanie having nine years worth of credit card madness to sort out — I did muster some tiny, temporary presence of mind to ask for a partnership. They agreed. *(Stephanie enters, a paper in her hand.)* I needed it on paper. I always need it on paper.

STEPHANIE.   Our partnership agreement ...

ORRIN.   *(Out.)* And a receipt for my hard-earned money. I always get a receipt.

RUSSELL.   Here you go. For ten big ones. *(Stephanie gives Orrin a Walkman, puts the earphones on his head.)*

STEPHANIE.   Now here, put these on ...

ORRIN.   *(Out.)* I was treated to a quick intensive in the *Strategies for Power* home seminar. *(Russell enters, piles a stack of books in his arms.)*

RUSSELL.   And read these.

ORRIN.   *(Out.)* I resisted it at first. I was accustomed to the vocabulary of my years studying in the groves of low-level academia ...

STEPHANIE.   I'd suggest you read them at least twice. Ideally, six or seven times.

ORRIN.   *(Out.)* This was a parallel universe; an alternate jargon which swung dizzily from the minutest of specifics, like:

RUSSELL.   *(Out.)* Make sure your post office box is centrally located.

ORRIN.   *(Out.)* And ...

STEPHANIE.   *(Out.)* A 1-800 number is indispensable.

ORRIN.   *(Out.)* ... To the incredibly general, such as ...

RUSSELL.   *(Out.)* To feel a true sense of worthiness with which to walk this world, you first must give yourself the gift of self-worth.

ORRIN.   *(Out.)* And ...

STEPHANIE.   *(Out.)* Power is an ever-available commodity. You can choose to harvest yours, and so have it continually replenish itself; or let it wither on the vine.

ORRIN.   *(Out.)* I found it maddening at first. The meat-and-potatoes advice seemed pedestrian at best, and the other stuff … well, unnecessarily metaphysical. And the metaphors were more than mixed; they were pureed. But it began to chip away at me anyway. I began to see that these quick shifts in scale and reference were the *very point,* wisely calculated to jolt us out of our — in uppercase, this is — our "Old-Brain Thinking." Especially with Russell and Stephanie there as guides, its truth started emerging for me, over time, in an increasingly bold relief.

RUSSELL. *(Out.)* You are limited only by the mental barbed wire you erect around your own life …

ORRIN. *(Out.)* … Russell would say, and I truly began to see the wisdom in this. Stephanie would add something like:

STEPHANIE. *(Out.)* The present moment is all there is.

ORRIN. *(Out.)* … And — particularly with Stephanie, because I was developing a wild crush on her — more on that later — but I soon took these concepts into my newly opened heart. *(Lights off Stephanie.)* Before too long, I had turned fully around and was employing *Strategies for Power* with equal zeal. And the material just kept coming over the transom! *(The UPS driver, Gail, enters, loaded down with tapes and books. Russell has made himself comfortable; has his shirt off already.)*

GAIL. Package for Russell Boam?

RUSSELL. Yes! Gina, is it?

GAIL. Gail. You guys sure do get a lot of these! You in a record club, or — ?

RUSSELL. Something *much* better. Thanks, Gail!

GAIL. Have a great day! *(She exits, cheerfully.)*

ORRIN. *(Out.)* But the theoretical would last only so long. *(Lights up on Stephanie and Russell, in the apartment.)*

STEPHANIE. This … is a time of gathering.

ORRIN. *(Out.)* It was time to begin the search for our widget, in earnest.

STEPHANIE. As with the seasons of the natural world, this time of gathering is limited.

ORRIN. *(Out.)* To that end, we huddled together for many sessions of what our operative jargon called "Imagination Slamming." *(Orrin joins their scene.)*

STEPHANIE.   So we've set a strict deadline for the end of this harvest season at four weeks from today. But —

RUSSELL.   But we don't worry about that right now. Right now we just slam and jam: throwing it out there, asking a shit-load of questions ...

STEPHANIE.   Right. But *the* question — the threshold question, from which all subset questions emerge — is — Russell?

RUSSELL.   *(Deliberately.)* What ... Do ... People ... *Want?*

STEPHANIE.   What Do People Want. If we don't lose track of that, we're going in the right direction. OK? Ready?

RUSSELL.   Ready, honey.

ORRIN.   Ready.

STEPHANIE.   Someone, of course, needs to serve; and someone needs to be ready to volley.

RUSSELL.   And we need a gear-switching mechanism.

STEPHANIE.   Correct. And for that, I suggest we apply the templates of "Micro" and "Macro."

ORRIN.   Oh ... What was that, again?

RUSSELL.   Very basic: Sequence One. You need to spend more time with the tapes, bud.

STEPHANIE.   Much more.

ORRIN.   Sorry.

STEPHANIE.   But let's not waste time explaining. Russell and I will get a flow going, you hitch a ride with it if you feel the movement.

ORRIN.   All right, Steph.

STEPHANIE.   And only if you feel it.

RUSSELL.   Meanwhile, you write down every single thing we say, whether it sounds visionary, or just fucking stupid.

ORRIN.   OK.

STEPHANIE.   You want me to start serving, honey?

RUSSELL.   Sure. And I take the Micro-slash-Macro gear switch responsibility?

STEPHANIE.   Yes.

RUSSELL.   Great. *(Dead silence. Everyone is waiting for someone else to follow procedure and say something. Finally.)*

STEPHANIE.   Russell, you're supposed to start. You ask me.

RUSSELL.   Oh! Don't you ask me to ask you?

STEPHANIE. That was optional, but — fine. Russell: Do you have a question to ask me?

RUSSELL. Yes I do, Stephanie: What Do People Want?

STEPHANIE. Oh ... Lots of things ...

RUSSELL. What is it, that people Want?

STEPHANIE. Many, many things ... Various and numerous things ... Umm ... A nice meal every now and then ... Storage space ... A good education ... A clean carpet ... Security ...

RUSSELL. Clarification! What kind of security, Steph? Give me the flavor ...

STEPHANIE. OK. Security from crime. From intrusion. Violence perpetrated on them. That's the track that I was —

RUSSELL. Light bulb! Micro: home security systems. Personal, portable protection devices. Self-defense seminars. Pepper-based spray, deployed against the eyes of the attacker.

ORRIN. Guns.

STEPHANIE. Keep it legal.

RUSSELL. Armored glass of some sort, for home or automobile ...

ORRIN. Guns can be legal.

RUSSELL. High-pitched, ultra-loud whistles which pierce through the attacker's very soul ...

STEPHANIE. I mean unfettered by any questions of lawfulness.

RUSSELL. Super-duper high-beam flashlights ...

STEPHANIE. Not worth the trouble. Been there, been there.

RUSSELL. Perhaps a flashlight which can double as a blunt striking instrument. — Anyone receiving this?

STEPHANIE. Sorry, honey.

RUSSELL. Fake security systems. Fake police sirens. Fake barking dogs. Fake male companions.

STEPHANIE. Been there, too.

RUSSELL. Steph, please ...

STEPHANIE. Sorry.

ORRIN. Fake male companions?

RUSSELL. Inflatable. Woman puts one in her window, maybe. Or in her passenger seat, for driving late at night. Big shoulders; big overhanging, simian brow; this brutish-looking —

STEPHANIE. — fucking *balloon*. Forget it. Home security's a glutted market, honey. Gear-switch back to Macro. The question again, please:

RUSSELL. What Do People *Want?*

ORRIN. *(Out.)* What I Wanted — what I Wanted most in the world, at this point — was Stephanie.

STEPHANIE. People Want:

ORRIN. *(Out.)* It needs to be said that this was not the first helpless crush I had embarked on. In some way, I could calibrate my life by its constant series of unrequited infatuations. Was this mature? Was this healthy? Undoubtedly not.

STEPHANIE. People Want: Brotherly love …

ORRIN. *(Out.)* But these crushes — nay, that's too weak: These tidal waves of love! — came so strong, and organized my world with such a sudden, merciless intensity, that I never obtained a proper perspective on the cyclical nature of my yearnings.

STEPHANIE. People Want: To be left alone …

ORRIN. *(Out.)* Which is to say, I didn't realize I was stepping into this shit again.

STEPHANIE. People Want: Their desks to be organized.

ORRIN. *(Out.)* But Stephanie! She was … special!

STEPHANIE. People Want: Better interpersonal communication.

ORRIN. *(Out.)* To me, she exuded an air of fallen nobility. Royalty in exile. A czarist princess, escaped from Russia. A doyenne of the Shang dynasty, thrown over by the Chou in eleventh-century B.C. China …

STEPHANIE. Imaging, imaging …

ORRIN. *(Out.)* Marie Antoinette, gliding with poise and grace on her way to the guillotine.

STEPHANIE. I'm drawing a fucking blank.

ORRIN. *(Out.)* With a perhaps slightly saltier vocabulary.

RUSSELL. Just relax, honey.

ORRIN. *(Out.)* I loved her rapid-fire intelligence; her white-hot anger; her occasional cast of deep sadness, which even came through all the *Strategies for Power* pep talk. I equated this sadness with depth.

STEPHANIE. Convenience in food shopping. A feeling of

community. Less fat in everything.

RUSSELL. Think more expansively.

STEPHANIE. Shut up, please.

ORRIN. *(Out.)* And perhaps as much as anything — and I say this with a bit of shame — I loved that Stephanie was not typical of the women Russell usually hooked up with, who tended to be virtual doormats for him.

STEPHANIE. Clothing that doesn't wrinkle.

ORRIN. *(Out.)* With Stephanie, his alpha status was far from certain. I took guilty delight in seeing his maddening ... confidence, shaken.

STEPHANIE. A feeling of ecological well-being in one's consumer choices.

ORRIN. *(Out.)* Soon, he confessed to me: *(Lights change quickly. A different scene: Russell and Orrin at a bar.)*

RUSSELL. I'm really off-balance with this one, buddy! She's a warrior. She's got the most formidable bullshit detector of any human I've ever met. She's been out there in the world; she's played hardball, while we were dinking around in the library, churning out meaningless papers on irrelevant topics ...

ORRIN. I ... I don't know about that, Russell. I think some of what I read about — the study of the Renaissance Popes, for just one example — isn't something that —

RUSSELL. You know where that woman has been? That phenomenal woman? She was fast track at a giant Wall Street law firm. Pow! Bam!

ORRIN. But they kicked her out.

RUSSELL. But it was because they couldn't get up to her speed; you know? They resented it. That's the kind of firepower we have working with us, in Stephanie. If she loses interest, this whole enterprise is toasted. *I* can't mess up with her, for that reason alone.

ORRIN. Russell, that's not a very good reason to —

RUSSELL. No no, you're right, yeah. But no: There's something else. I ... I don't know myself anymore, Orrin. This one is different; Stephanie's different. I ... I think I'm in love with her. You ever hear me say that before?

ORRIN. No.

24

RUSSELL. No, I didn't think I did. But I am, I am in love with her! Shit, just saying that! What a buzz! I am *in* love with Stephanie! I love her! Yeah!

ORRIN. Boy.

RUSSELL. Or, I'm just scared shitless of her.

ORRIN. Boy.

RUSSELL. Maybe both!

ORRIN. *(Out.)* I was touched by Russell's genuine confusion; it was so … rare, in him. But as the Imagination Slams continued day after day, I was tortured by my wide-open heart. To be fair, I think they had no idea, as I am classically long-suffering and silent in my pain. But often the situation bordered on cruel; as when — following the *Strategies for Power* dictum that one works whenever one feels the energy bubble up — they'd call me to come over for a late-night Imagination Slam. At times, these sessions were — how should I say this? — at times these sessions were clearly … post-coital. *(Russell, Stephanie in bed, naked under the covers. Orrin in a chair nearby, with his pad and pencil.)*

RUSSELL. An easy way of making fresh orange juice … A way of ascertaining the loyalty of a friend …

ORRIN. *(Out.)* This was painful.

RUSSELL. More flexibility to … clean their homes … without cleaning … Strike that one. All-purpose shoes.

STEPHANIE. Micro! A sneaker which converts to a dress shoe. A dress shoe which converts to a sort of slipper. A slipper which metamorphosizes into a version of a quasi-hiking boot. — Shit, that's pathetic! Strike all that, too!

RUSSELL. We're censoring ourselves too much.

STEPHANIE. Our deadline's tomorrow. It's time to weed out the crap!

RUSSELL. Not until then, however. This is just a gathering of —

STEPHANIE. And our Macro-slash-Micro distinctions are getting dangerously blurry, in my opinion. Not to mention stupid. — I'm taking a shower. *(Stephanie gets out of bed, making only a minimal effort to cover herself. Orrin is hyper-alert to this.)* "All-purpose shoes," God! *(Notices Orrin.)* What are you looking at?

ORRIN.   Nothing, Steph.

STEPHANIE.   I'll never understand the big fuss men make over tits. Some fatty tissue, a nipple. Big fucking deal. *(Exits.)*

RUSSELL.   Jesus! She's too much.

ORRIN.   *(Out.)* Our self-imposed deadline was zooming up, and making us all very tense.

RUSSELL.   Too much! She can really be ... out of control, at times.

ORRIN.   *(Out.)* There was nothing that truly had, in the parlance of *Strategies for Power,* "opened the door" for us, catapulting us to that new level.

RUSSELL.   And that's why — you know. It was inevitable.

ORRIN.   *(Out.)* The *Strategies* also said not to set up an actual office until you've gone through that door; so we were still working in Stephanie's apartment. Which, for obvious reasons, I could have done without.

RUSSELL.   It's how I'm wired.

ORRIN.   *(Out.)* But there was another undercurrent.

RUSSELL.   It's biology. I can't apologize for my biology! In the face of my love for Stephanie — which is powerful. In the face of the very real fear I have of her — also powerful — I cannot help myself.

ORRIN.   Who is she?

RUSSELL.   Some girl with big green eyes who works the desk at my health club. We've been in flirtation mode for weeks; finally it came to its natural fruition. We hooked up last night, at her place.

ORRIN.   God, Russell! I mean, Stephanie — !

RUSSELL.   I know, I know! Jesus Christ, maybe I'm just scum, I don't know. But I can't go forward — live, relate with people, and function — on the premise of myself being scum, you know?

ORRIN.   You could try it for a while, anyway!

RUSSELL.   No, it must be how I'm wired. 'Cause I swore to myself, up and down, that I'd be monogamous with Steph, when we first got serious — and I was, buddy, remember! For eight months!

ORRIN.   Oh, *please,* Russell!

RUSSELL. It's an absolute record for me, though! Of which I'm genuinely proud! But the more we get entangled in the nuts and bolts of this business together …

ORRIN. This enterprise …

RUSSELL. Right, the more we get entreprenurially en-meshed … the more the sexual energy seems to need a re-rout-ing. You know?

ORRIN. No, I don't know! I'm sorry, I don't think you can justify it so easily! You're … lying!

RUSSELL. I know, I know. It's fucking juvenile! And you know what, buddy? You're 100% right.

ORRIN. About what?

RUSSELL. I'm going to cut it out. Totally. You're right, it's heinous. Pointless. Icky. I'm not going to repeat this act of self-destruction.

ORRIN. I think that's a good idea, Russell. If you want my opinion.

RUSSELL. I do! I most definitely do! God, Orrin! You're great. You're the best! You're golden!

ORRIN. No I'm not.

RUSSELL. You are! You cut through to the heart of an issue better than anyone sometimes. You're the voice of pure moral-ity.

ORRIN. Jesus, no I'm not. Not at all. I just —

RUSSELL. Do me a favor. If you see me going off the rails again — even if it just seems like a *potential* derailment — throw some cold water in my face. Ream me a new asshole. I'm ask-ing you to, as a friend.

ORRIN. I don't know if I want to ream you a —

RUSSELL. Please! I'm begging you. I'd consider it one of the kindest things you could do for me.

ORRIN. Well … I guess.

RUSSELL. Thank you, Orrin! You're a good friend. A man of Quality. My *best* friend.

ORRIN. I'll try.

RUSSELL. I'll do the same for you! Should you find yourself in this situation.

ORRIN. *(Lights off Russell. Out.)* That last bit was gratuitous.

Being as unlikely as it was. I wasn't that adventurous. Nor was I the moral rock-of-ages that Russell imagined I was. It was more a difference of temperament, doled out by the gods at birth. So he may have been right: It may indeed have been in the way we were "wired." I was slower. Plodding. Sluggish, even. I moved cautiously, examining each step, doubting each footprint behind me. Russell and Stephanie were given to acceleration; immediate release. Torrid declarations; sudden, athletic and all-consuming sex; bold, zealous, but often touchingly innocent pronouncements about — in uppercase, this is — The Way We Live Now. Myself, I preferred staying inside and reading. More than anything else, I still loved reading history. At that time, I retained my dream of teaching it someday, once the world was in the mood to employ teachers again. After a heavy concentration on the Middle Ages in grad school, I had recently rolled the calendar even further back, just on a whim, for my own nutty enjoyment, and before I knew it got heavily immersed in the Ancients. The original Dead White Males: the Greeks. I was fascinated by the story of Solon, a chief magistrate of Athens in the sixth-century B.C. Solon was chosen to save the land during an era of crisis: After centuries of bloody injustice, things were about to boil over. But by the time he was in office for a while he had abolished slavery for the indebted, established voting rights for peasants, and generally extended civil rights much further than had ever been seen before. I don't mean to canonize the guy: He was a man of his time. Some of his reforms were just plain weird — like his law requiring husbands to have sex with their wives at least three times a month, or get thrown in jail. What was *that* about? But on the whole, he was so wise and so popular that he was asked to intensify his absolute control of Athens by accepting the title of Tyrant. Uppercase T; Tyrant. "Please, be our Tyrant!" they begged. And an amazing, unprecedented, thing happened: He turned it down! *(Spot off Orrin. Lights up on Russell, sitting alone in the apartment wearing only his boxer shorts, a Walkman and earphones on, eyes closed, reciting by rote.)*
RUSSELL.   I am a warrior. I walk through fire unscathed. Time and distance mean nothing to me. They are but illusions.

I kill when I must but use what I kill. My spirit is ever expanding. *(Enter the UPS Driver, Gail, carrying a package. She knocks lightly; waits patiently to be noticed.)* My spirit is ever expanding. I am a warrior. I walk through fire unscathed. Time and distance mean nothing to me. They — *(Gail clears her throat. Russell opens his eyes.)* Hello!

GAIL. Hi.

RUSSELL. Affirmations. Native American based, really state of the art. Path to power. Completely cool.

GAIL. They sound very nice. Another package for Russell Boam?

RUSSELL. *C'est moi.* More tapes from our network. *(He takes the package.)* Your name again? Gloria?

GAIL. Gail.

RUSSELL. Gail! Excuse my ... bareness. Gail.

GAIL. Seems you dress like that a lot.

RUSSELL. It helps me think. To shed some layers.

GAIL. I don't really care. I grew up with five brothers. All sorts of things swinging around the house.

RUSSELL. That's cute.

GAIL. Thank you.

RUSSELL. You're cute.

GAIL. Thanks. — Would you ... sign, please, sir?

RUSSELL. Gladly. *(He signs.)* Let me ask you something. You have a couple seconds?

GAIL. Not too many, actually.

RUSSELL. I don't need many. Just — without thinking at all, whatever pops into your head — just answer this simple question: What is it that people ... *Want?*

GAIL. "Want?"

RUSSELL. To make them happy.

GAIL. Um. Why?

RUSSELL. Doesn't matter. Just off the top of your head. "People Want — "

GAIL. People want ... I don't know. *Niceness.*

RUSSELL. "Niceness"?

GAIL. I'm sorry.

RUSSELL. Don't apologize! Just do me this favor, be more specific. Anything: a look, a smell; the flavor of this "niceness" …

GAIL.   Um. Anything! Anywhere you look. There's where I find it. I look for it, then it's there. God, that's really corny, sorry. But … it's true. I think.

RUSSELL.   Where do you think most people look? For niceness?

GAIL.   To each other? A … friendly face?

RUSSELL.   And…?

GAIL.   And to … soft things? I'm sorry, I don't express myself too well.

RUSSELL.   How do you express yourself best?

GAIL.   I like to draw. It's what I want to do, in life. Art.

RUSSELL.   Hey, art's great.

GAIL.   I'm always drawing. Sketching. Even when I'm doing deliveries, I almost get into car crashes 'cause I'm always peering out to see things spatially; their texture? And you know, the way they're arranged dimensionally? And definitely in terms of color. And —

RUSSELL.   Here … A napkin, a pen. Draw it for me. Draw —

GAIL.   My truck's double-parked.

RUSSELL.   Just quickly! Draw me the "niceness." The friendly face. The softness.

GAIL.   Well … *(As she draws.)* Why do you want this?

RUSSELL.   We have a deadline here tomorrow. I'm trying to re-route my thinking.

GAIL.   Oh.

RUSSELL.   Plus, I'm a student of people. Especially people I instinctively like.

GAIL.   Thank you. — Here. Pretty silly.

RUSSELL.   No, it's lovely. An … animal?

GAIL.   I guess. Maybe. Kind of a … little critter, I guess. Smiling out at everyone.

RUSSELL.   But not too cloyingly. Just … right. I love this! It's exactly what you said! It is!

GAIL.   I guess. Sorry, I have to go, sir.

RUSSELL.   Can I take you out to dinner? To thank you?

GAIL.   I don't know.

RUSSELL.   Don't you find me attractive?

GAIL.   I sort of … do. But I don't think so. My truck —

RUSSELL.   Later, I mean. Please …

GAIL.   I'm not sure it would be —

RUSSELL.   I'll put on some pants first, I promise.

GAIL.   Well …

RUSSELL.   *(He catches himself.)* Wait. Sorry. This is reflexive. Old-Brain. I'm being a jerk. Never mind. I swore not to do this stuff. Forgive me. I'm attached. To a great woman. *(He starts putting on his clothes.)*

GAIL.   Then you definitely shouldn't do this stuff.

RUSSELL.   You're right. Everybody's right.

GAIL.   Who is? Huh?

RUSSELL.   You ever meet her on a delivery? Stephanie? She works here.

GAIL.   No. Just you. Oh — and does another man work here?

RUSSELL.   Theoretically. *(Hands her a picture from his wallet.)* This is her.

GAIL.   Oh, she's beautiful!

RUSSELL.   She is, isn't she?

GAIL.   I'd love to look like her! God, you shouldn't let her go!

RUSSELL.   You're right. Sorry, this is … embarrassing.

GAIL.   Well … You kinda did the right thing. Eventually.

RUSSELL.   I did, didn't I? Good for me!

GAIL.   'Bye.

RUSSELL.   Again, my apologies.

GAIL.   It's OK. I have to go. Have a nice day! *(Gail exits. Russell looks closely at the drawing.)*

RUSSELL.   "Nice." "Niceness." *(Lights shift. A new scene: Russell shows the drawing to Stephanie and Orrin.)*

STEPHANIE.   What … is it?

RUSSELL.   It's simplicity. A few simple lines and curves. It's what we kept avoiding.

STEPHANIE.   Is it a dog?

RUSSELL.   One of the *Strategy's* Prime Directives: Keep It Elemental.

STEPHANIE.   A bear?

RUSSELL.   We jumped into the breach of specificity far too early for our own good.

ORRIN.   A cat, I think.

RUSSELL.   If you want it to be, young man!

STEPHANIE.   Kind of an anthropomorphized dog-bear-cute little elf-kitty-cat-sort of marsupial-Casper the Friendly Ghost-hippopotamus-vague caricature of Buddy Hackett-panda-Hobbit-like thing. Bit of Winston Churchill, in there too.

ORRIN.   A … cartoon.

RUSSELL.   Is there … shame, in that?

ORRIN.   I … don't think so.

RUSSELL.   Your voice betrayed some shame.

ORRIN.   No it didn't.

RUSSELL.   Some … disappointment, at least?

ORRIN.   I'm sorry if it did, Russell.

RUSSELL.   Because the threshold question applicable here is —

STEPHANIE.   "How Does It Make You *Feel?*"

RUSSELL.   Precisely! God, I love you! I love you, Stephanie! I love her, Orrin! She's my lover! You're my lover.

STEPHANIE.   I know, honey.

RUSSELL.   I love you!

STEPHANIE.   "How Does It Make You Feel?" Hmmm. *(She studies it, hard.)*

RUSSELL.   Well?

STEPHANIE.   Well … If I were to simply catch it out of the corner of my eye one day …

RUSSELL.   Right, right …

STEPHANIE.   Trying hard here to gear-switch from the mode of scrutiny I'm naturally in right now, that is, as a person who could potentially be in business for years selling a fucking cartoon …

RUSSELL.   Right, good; switch the gears; grind 'em if you have to …

STEPHANIE.   I'd have to say … It would make me feel …

RUSSELL.   Yeah?

STEPHANIE.   *Nice.* Yes: "Nice."

RUSSELL.   Bull's-eye!

STEPHANIE.   It's playful, it connotes innocence, without coming on too sugary-sweet. I mean, it's not reaching out putting

32

its hands into your fucking liver, massaging it, gratuituously …

RUSSELL.   Which is a bad thing, right?

STEPHANIE.   Right. It's affectionate, but knowing … Something in the expression … accommodates a lot.

RUSSELL.   Yes!

ORRIN.   I'm starting to see more dog, now.

RUSSELL.   Good!

STEPHANIE.   I see what you're getting at, baby … It's a tabula rasa. It — he, she, or it — suggests a feeling, but from there is infinitely pliable …

RUSSELL.   Well put, Steph!

STEPHANIE.   And so the market could — potentially — come to it, rather than it having to go to market! Sequence Five, Volume Three, Chapter Twenty-Seven!

RUSSELL.   Right!

STEPHANIE.   This is … *it!*

RUSSELL.   Yes!

STEPHANIE.   I really think this is it!

RUSSELL.   I think it is! It's it!

STEPHANIE.   Do you feel the door opening, too, honey?

RUSSELL.   I do! *(They kiss: very long, very passionately.)*

RUSSELL.   God, I love you!

STEPHANIE.   I love you, too!

RUSSELL.   I love you so much! *(They kiss again: longer, harder; hands groping. Orrin tries not to watch. Finally they come up for air.)* I love you! *(Stephanie turns to Orrin, smiling.)*

STEPHANIE.   Orrin? What about you?

ORRIN.   I — ! Well, I also —

STEPHANIE.   About the door opening?

ORRIN.   Oh! Right.

RUSSELL.   Buddy? The partnership's already in two-thirds agreement, so we don't really need your stamp. But unanimity would be a superb energy to start with.

ORRIN.   *(Out.)* What could I say? She was looking right into my eyes, beaming!

STEPHANIE.   Orrin?

ORRIN.   I … God, I — I love it!

RUSSELL.   All RIGHT! *(Russell steers himself and Stephanie over*

as a unit. They swoop in on Orrin, and engulf him in an embrace.)
STEPHANIE.   We did it! *(She kisses Orrin.)*
RUSSELL.   The three of us! *(They dance around wildly as a three-some; then break off into individual victory dances.)*
ORRIN.   *(Out.)* "The three of us!" We were euphoric! The three of us! All doubt, all jealousy, melted away for the present moment … Everything that seemed complicated and tortured suddenly was not. I was connected!
STEPHANIE.   The door is opened!
RUSSELL.   We opened the door!
ORRIN.   Yeah! That … door! It got opened!
RUSSELL.   Spike the ball!
STEPHANIE.   Eureka!
RUSSELL.   Kill the fatted calf, baby! *(Stephanie takes another look, admiring it.)*
STEPHANIE.   Russell? Who drew it?
RUSSELL.   Well … I … I did.
STEPHANIE.   Honey! Really!
RUSSELL.   Yup. Me. *(Music cranks up. Blackout.)*

END OF ACT ONE

ACT TWO

Spot on Orrin.

ORRIN.   *(Out.)* Once Solon sailed to Lydia to visit the very wealthy King Croesus. You know, as in the expression "rich as Croesus." As they got loaded on wine one night, Croesus declared himself, quote, "the happiest man alive," unquote. Solon politely begged to differ, saying — in essence — that these were just words; and that words were slippery: that all Croesus' vast wealth would not necessarily keep him something called "happy." Croesus flew into a drunken rage at having his assertion challenged; they parted on nasty terms. But years later, when Croesus' kingdom had grown even more decadent and corrupt — Croesus, by the way, had spent a treasure trove of wealth and words to assure himself that he had in fact not become decadent and corrupt — his luck turned. And — classically — Croesus was shocked by this turn of events. And when he was taken prisoner by the Persians, and sat atop a pyre ready to be burned — he cried out Solon's name. *(Stephanie and Russell appear in dim light.)*
STEPHANIE.   Paulie.
ORRIN.   With his last breath, he called out for the Athenian's hard-won wisdom.
STEPHANIE.   Paula.
RUSSELL.   Papa. *(Lights up on their brand-new office. Stephanie, Russell, Orrin are all dressed in their business best now. They pace: a rapid-fire Imagination Slam.)*
STEPHANIE.   Peter, Petey, Piltdown, Pippy …
RUSSELL.   Pin-Head, Priscilla, Pooky, Poo-Bah — "Poo-Bah!" I kind of like that.
STEPHANIE.   Too much like Pooh-Bear. Have fucking Christopher Robin's estate on your ass in no time.
RUSSELL.   Right.
STEPHANIE.   Pug, Puggy, Puttyhead …
ORRIN.   Prong.
RUSSELL.   Jesus, Orrin! "Prong"?

ORRIN. Sorry.

STEPHANIE. Peppy, Pesty ...

ORRIN. Pimples.

STEPHANIE. "Pimples"? Yuck.

RUSSELL. Let's try to keep focused.

STEPHANIE. This is a terrible use of time, honey.

RUSSELL. Pally, Patty, Poppy, Puff-ball, Peeble, Peabo ...

STEPHANIE. Popo, Pobo, Poco, Polo, Pozzo — too Italianate, all of them.

RUSSELL. Move on to the "R"s.

STEPHANIE. Ralph, Rascal ...

ORRIN. *(Out.)* We embarked on the next phase: An actual office was rented! The first thing we did there was have a desperate Mini-Slam for two days.

STEPHANIE. Rebecca, Robby ...

ORRIN. *(Out.)* Forty-eight hours of non-stop nomenclature for our new critter. A trying Slam indeed.

RUSSELL. Rolo, Rocky, Rockwell ...

STEPHANIE. Rockefeller, Ruffles ...

RUSSELL. Ruffles!

STEPHANIE. Goddamned potato chip.

RUSSELL. Raymond, Raphael, Reggie ...

STEPHANIE. Ricky, Rimsky-Korsakov, Rubby, Rumpus ...

ORRIN. *(Out.)* Until finally Russell had a Lightbulb:

RUSSELL. Russell!

STEPHANIE. You're kidding.

RUSSELL. No! Look, I'm not trying to immortalize myself, but think of its virtues: It's a dignified-sounding name, but not pompous. It passes our Muppet test ... Can't you see a fucking Muppet with that name?

STEPHANIE. They don't have a "Russell?"

RUSSELL. I don't believe they do. And in case it does evolve into a more specific creature, zoologically-speaking, it can go a lot of ways, in terms of alliteration: Russell the Rabbit, Russell the Raccoon, I don't know ... Russell the Rodent...!

ORRIN. Russell the Robot. *(They look at him, incredulous.)* With ... hair.

RUSSELL. You are a very odd young man.

36

ORRIN.   No, I mean, I like it!

STEPHANIE.   Fine by me. It's all in the thing's look and feel. After that, you can name it "Stalin."

ORRIN.   *(Out.)* "Russell" it was. This was in fact a diversion, though; a subset Slam, from the main avenue of imaginative inquiry: How to Market Your Widget. *(Slight light change: another strategy session.)*

STEPHANIE.   We fax the thing all over God's green acre. The prototype.

RUSSELL.   On the napkin, you mean.

STEPHANIE.   Yes. Fax the shit out of it; all over the planet. Sequence Seven: Casting Your Bread on the Waters.

RUSSELL.   Yes!

ORRIN.   *(Out.)* So we faxed the um, shit out of it. To:

STEPHANIE.   Toy manufacturers; soft drink bottlers; all packagers of breakfast cereal that could use an adorable spokesthing …

RUSSELL.   Comic book publishers; clothing designers …

STEPHANIE.   Bubble gum card makers; animation companies; software makers …

ORRIN.   Schools …

RUSSELL.   They can't do a thing for us, buddy …

STEPHANIE.   Sports Teams lacking a suitable mascot …

RUSSELL.   Beer; Tires … Can't you see cute little Russell behind the wheel of a car, doing a hundred fifty miles an hour?

STEPHANIE.   Looking completely unfazed and serene despite the speed; absolutely!

RUSSELL.   Major utility companies; stationary manufacturers.

STEPHANIE.   Fast food!

RUSSELL.   Fast food!

STEPHANIE.   Fast food! Yes! *(They begin to kiss passionately. Soon their hands are all over each other.)*

ORRIN.   *(Out.)* As per our new *Strategies for Power* Advanced Evolution Sequences Tapes and Supporting Materials, we dove into the recommended Guerrilla Marketing Campaign. The idea works thusly: Once you have a solid idea …

RUSSELL.   *(Out.)* … But not so specific as to cramp unforeseen opportunities …

STEPHANIE. *(Out.)* ... You flood the universe with it. You fully expect your backwash will be a low percentage of this flood, but even this will be a steady, flowing, crystal-clear stream.

ORRIN. *(Out.)* We followed the *Strategies'* advice to the letter, including the whole separate bonus cassette we received:

STEPHANIE. *(Out.)* "Cultivating the Sphinx Within." It says to withhold just enough — to whet appetites, then pull back ...

RUSSELL. *(Out.)* Coyly. Flirt with 'em. Leave 'em hard up.

STEPHANIE. *(Out.)* Give 'em blue balls. Needing further information about your widget.

ORRIN. *(Out.)* To this end:

STEPHANIE. *(Out.)* Proliferation! Thousands of faxes, popping up unexpectedly all over the world. With just this: the prototype of little Russell, Jr. ... and one simple caption underneath: "Let Me Be Your Partner." Inviting, but not too touchy-feeley. Then our 1-800 number!

ORRIN. *(Out.)* Stephanie! ... oh, she was in rare form in this period! She was a ... virtuoso! An entrepreneurial Rembrandt. Our new office had awakened a sleeping giant in her! Russell and I could only watch in awe. And when push came to shove in any matter of *Strategies* interpretation, she was always deferred to. For good reason: She got results. *(Slight light change: another office scene. Russell runs in, waving papers.)*

RUSSELL. Look at this! Today alone, sixty-five reply faxes!

STEPHANIE. Two-point-five times better than we hoped!

RUSSELL. I love you! You still love me?

STEPHANIE. I do! *(They kiss; soon their hands are all over each other. As Stephanie caresses his chest, she feels something in his shirt pocket.)*

STEPHANIE. What's ... this?

RUSSELL. Oh ... Just ... *(She fishes it out.)*

STEPHANIE. A ... condom. My, my.

RUSSELL. Yes.

STEPHANIE. My, my. Um. What's it doing — ?

RUSSELL. For us.

STEPHANIE. Hm. Yes, but ... we have hundreds of them at the apartment.

RUSSELL. I just … Just in case … Sometime … We want to, here …

STEPHANIE. Really?

RUSSELL. I thought it might be nice sometime, once Orrin's gone home…?

STEPHANIE. Have sex here in the office?

RUSSELL. Yeah.

STEPHANIE. Well … It's a very sweet thought, but … Russell? I don't know how to say this any way but directly: You're not … lying to me, are you, Russell?

RUSSELL. No!

STEPHANIE. I get massive headaches when I'm being lied to. I can't take it. OK?

RUSSELL. I understand, honey. Me either. And I won't. I'm not.

STEPHANIE. Good. Thank you.

RUSSELL. You trust me?

STEPHANIE. *(Pause. A choice.)* Yes. I do. *(Lights shift: Russell and Orrin at the bar.)*

ORRIN. You said you were going to cut this out!

RUSSELL. I'm still in the process of changing. We all need a learning curve, buddy! And my incidents *have* gone way down, frequency-wise. Pretty soon I'll be at zero.

ORRIN. Disgusting!

RUSSELL. Thanks for your support, Best Friend.

ORRIN. You told me to! You said to ream you a new asshole!

RUSSELL. You could do it more gently. I mean, that was … nerve-wracking! Her finding that in my pocket!

ORRIN. Who was it for?

RUSSELL. Some brown-eyed shoestore clerk I'd been doing a banter with for almost two years — before I even met Steph! Yeah, it pre-dates my monogamy, so that might be a factor: Maybe that just achieved its natural, inevitable little closure, and now it's over. I won't repeat it. OK?

ORRIN. I … guess. But … I don't have to like it.

RUSSELL. That is your absolute right and privilege as an autonomous human being, yes. But … a little sympathy, buddy? *(Lights off Russell.)*

39

ORRIN.   *(Out.)* I had none. He was squandering a treasure. And I knew that this poison would soon seep into the air at the office, dense as smoke. *(Lights up on the office: Stephanie is pissed; Russell sits there looking exhausted.)*

STEPHANIE.   We need more than one fucking dirty napkin!

ORRIN.   *(Out.)* It led us all to speaking in a sort of code.

STEPHANIE.   So — what? — you had one moment of magic? Is that it?

RUSSELL.   I've tried, honey.

STEPHANIE.   We now have requests for Russell — the *cute* Russell — in different mileus. This is what we hoped for, and now we have it. And you're telling me you had one little visit from your muse, never to be so graced again?

RUSSELL.   I've been working all night to —

STEPHANIE.   They're not even close! Little bunches of … scribble! Look, this one looks like a deranged cow, this is just a blob, this one's some grotesque fucking Munchkin — and what's this, J. Edgar Hoover with half his face melted?! It's the art therapy of a sociopath!

RUSSELL.   You do it, then!

STEPHANIE.   I can't! I never said I could! You did!

RUSSELL.   Fine! We'll just scrap it, then! Sell cheapo burglar alarms, or giant gumball machines! Buy into some skanky frozen yogurt franchise! Nice and safe, and incredibly fucking finite!

STEPHANIE.   That's not the point! You introduced this to us, we hitched onto your vision, opened a door together, hooray hooray hooray; you said you drew it …

RUSSELL.   I'm sorry that you can't bring yourself to trust me! *(He bolts to his feet, exits.)*

STEPHANIE.   Fucking JERK.

ORRIN.   *(Out.)* I wanted to let her weep on my shoulder. I was sending signals: "He's not worthy of you. Take solace with me, the man who truly loves you."

STEPHANIE.   Wants me to trust him.

ORRIN.   *(Out.)* One does not voluntarily step in front of a speeding truck. When I … smiled at her, I thought it was a comforting smile.

STEPHANIE.   How could he do this to me?

ORRIN.   *(Out.)* I suppose I was not aware of the real quality to that particular ... cast, to my face.

STEPHANIE.   Jesus! Are you just going to ... stare at me, Orrin?

ORRIN.   *(Caught off guard.)* Wh — What, Steph?

STEPHANIE.   I'm getting pretty tired of you, leering at me all the time! Don't think I haven't noticed!

ORRIN.   I — I haven't meant to, you know, leer at you, Steph. I'm sorry.

STEPHANIE.   And who said you could call me "Steph?" Do I call you "Or?" "Golly gee, OR, it's time to slop the hogs ..."

RUSSELL.   Sorry. I heard Russell say it, and —

STEPHANIE.   He's my lover! We sleep together. And I barely tolerated it from him at first. But ... Now it's come to mean something. It's ... We ... We're ... lovers.

ORRIN.   Sorry, Steph. Anie. *(Awkward pause.)* Can I get you anything? A sparkling water? We have both fruit essence, and plain. You want a sparkling water?

STEPHANIE.   No thank you. *(Pause. She puts her head in her hands. Orrin watches. She looks up, pissed.)* What? Stop looking at me like a needy little puppy dog! Have some fucking self-respect, will you, Orrin?

ORRIN.   Sorry.

STEPHANIE.   What do you want me to do? Just turn around and say, "Come here, stud, you'll do just as well!"

ORRIN.   What — what are you talking about?

STEPHANIE.   Oh, please! I'm not blind! I even allowed for the fact that I might be a complete egomaniac, at first. But no. The way you ... stare. You clearly have some ... thing, for me. Right?

ORRIN.   Jesus, Stephanie ... No!

STEPHANIE.   Please, let's be real. You do, don't you?

ORRIN.   I ... might. OK.

STEPHANIE.   Well, forget it! It's too late. You should have done something about it, way back when we first met. You just rolled over, and showed your belly. Let Russell have what he wants.

ORRIN. But — God, I can't believe you're — ! Weren't you more attracted to him?

STEPHANIE. No. Well ... All right, in this case, perhaps, yes, for the initial impression at least. But that doesn't matter.

ORRIN. Oh, I happen to think it does! A lot!

STEPHANIE. But you didn't even expend the effort! And you never have. At least he did. So I can never think of you like you want me to, OK? Russell thought me worth *risking* something. To me, right now, yes, he's a fucking scumbag ... But at least he tries to show up on the radar!

ORRIN. I'm sorry that I'm so ... irrelevant! I just happened to like you!

STEPHANIE. Big deal.

ORRIN. To love you!

STEPHANIE. And so — what? I owe you something, now?

ORRIN. Civility, at least!

STEPHANIE. Please, don't go feeling sorry for yourself, honey.

ORRIN. *(Sputtering.)* You...! You...! You have no right to speak to me like that!

STEPHANIE. Ohhh ... Get away from me, please, Orrin. I'm not in the mood.

ORRIN. We are no longer friends! We are — !

STEPHANIE. You mean we were? Most of my friends don't just gawk at me like a psycho all day.

ORRIN. Don't you — ! Don't you say that! Don't you say that!

STEPHANIE. You're just proving my point, doing that! Leave me alone, Orrin. You're in my grief space!

ORRIN. Don't you — ! Don't you — ! Don't you dare — !

STEPHANIE. Go AWAY! *(He backs away. Lights down on Stephanie.)*

ORRIN. *(Out.)* I now *hated* Stephanie for doing that to me! She was heartless and cruel! So ... no one was really speaking to anyone, at this point. Morale sank lower and lower, headed for the sharp rocks below. *(Spot on Gail, smiling. In civilian clothes this time.)*

GAIL. My name's Gail.

ORRIN. *(Out.)* Then through our rapidly closing door walked a breath of fresh spring air. Sorry for this mixed metaphor of my own, but you get what I mean. *(Light shift: the office. Russell joins Gail.)*

RUSSELL.   Sorry, what do I keep calling you?

GAIL.   Grace.

RUSSELL.   Whoa. Paging Dr. Freud. *(They both laugh.)* Sorry, Gail.

GAIL.   You really went all out to track me down.

RUSSELL.   When it's worth the effort, you expend it. Damn-the-torpedoes kinda thing.

GAIL.   Your partners want to hire someone, too?

RUSSELL.   I need Stephanie's OK, at least. But yeah, we have an increasingly urgent situation here.

GAIL.   To have a job, just drawing! So great! It's so — !

RUSSELL.   Gail. I want to remind you. First we have to understand —

GAIL.   Wow! It's a dream come true!

RUSSELL.   Gail! Please, this is important: *(He comes closer; talks sotto voce.)* We do understand each other clearly, don't we? You will keep mum about doing the prototype?

GAIL.   Proto-what?

RUSSELL.   On the napkin. This is crucial, now, Gail.

GAIL.   Oh! Right.

RUSSELL.   Like I said, I panicked, and told them I did it.

GAIL.   Tsk. Shame on you.

RUSSELL.   I know. I'm really an adolescent at heart. But that happens to be the situation we're stuck with. Can you do me that favor?

GAIL.   I don't know … I think that possibly —

RUSSELL.   Wait — actually, I actually have to do *myself* the favor of reiterating it this way, Gail. Actually, you MUST do me that favor. If you want this job. OK?

GAIL.   Wow.

RUSSELL.   Remember, "Parsons."

GAIL.   Umm … What?

RUSSELL.   Ssshhh. *(Enter Stephanie: brisk, all business.)*

STEPHANIE.   Hello.

RUSSELL.   And we're looking awfully cheery today!

STEPHANIE.   Don't give me any shit. I've had a headache for three days straight. — My name's Stephanie Rommel.

GAIL.   Gail. Gail Myszlewski. It's really a pleasure to — !

STEPHANIE.   We're all kind of crabby here these days, Gail. Don't let it bother you. Russell says you just graduated from Parsons School of Design?

GAIL.   Oh! Yes!

STEPHANIE.   And you can draw the cute little thingie-wingie?

GAIL.   Yes, I think I can.

STEPHANIE.   Let's see. Here's the prototype. A bit disgusting after the last month's wear and tear, but try to look past the coffee stains. Here's some paper. First, just copy it.

GAIL.   All right.

ORRIN.   *(Out.)* Russell told me that he and Stephanie had made a sort of provisional truce.

GAIL.   Here.

STEPHANIE.   Quick. And good.

ORRIN.   *(Out.)* Since we were losing our momentum, he would scour New York's art schools …

STEPHANIE.   … *Very* good. Now, quick as you can, give me a few embellishments: um, Little Russell playing basketball …

ORRIN.   *(Out.)* … To try to find someone who might have the right touch.

STEPHANIE.   Quicker this time! Little Russell in a tuxedo; a James Bond look — God, when will this headache go away? *(Gail sketches rapidly, hands it back.)* Now Little Russell as a … whatever, a blacksmith … *(Gail again works quickly, hands it back.)*

GAIL.   Here!

STEPHANIE.   Now little Russell … oh, I don't know … on the fucking Supreme Court …

GAIL.   Great! *(Again, Gail works, hands it back.)*

STEPHANIE.   Very, *very* good. You even got in a few of the others — that's Rehnquist, isn't it?

GAIL.   The main guy, with the weird head. Yes. And that's a giant fuzzy gavel!

STEPHANIE.   Superb. You're a whiz!

GAIL.   Thank you.

44

STEPHANIE.   You're hired.

GAIL.   Great! Thank you!

RUSSELL.   All right! Score!

ORRIN.   *(Out.)* My pent-up feelings for Stephanie needed somewhere else to live, having been so rudely evicted.

STEPHANIE.   I'll draw you up a contract tonight. Hourly wage. We'll try to give you what you need.

RUSSELL.   Pretty damn good recruiting, huh Steph?

STEPHANIE.   Sure, sure. Let's get right to work.

GAIL.   This is great! *(Orrin enters the scene.)*

RUSSELL.   Orrin! This is Gail. She works here, as of ... thirty seconds ago!

ORRIN.   Hello.

GAIL.   Hi Orrin. It's so nice to meet you! God, this is great! I can't believe — God! I'm in shock! Some days everything just goes so great!

STEPHANIE.   I need some aspirin.

ORRIN.   *(Out.)* Gail! She was ... special! I watched as she threw herself heart and soul into *Strategies for Power* ... *(Lights shift: Russell gives Gail a Walkman, puts headphones on her.)*

RUSSELL.   Here, put these on ...

GAIL.   Great! *(Russell piles books in her arms.)*

RUSSELL.   And read these.

GAIL.   Thank you!

ORRIN.   *(Out.)* She found it ... great!

GAIL.   It's great!

RUSSELL.   We suggest you read them at least nine or ten times.

GAIL.   Great!

ORRIN.   *(Out.)* As days went on, Stephanie receded further into a darkness where no one dared follow ...

STEPHANIE.   *(Out.)* I need some goddamned ibuprofen.

ORRIN.   *(Out.)* But Gail was charmingly oblivious to it all!

GAIL.   *(Out.)* I love this job! And this material really speaks to me! It's true, the present moment *is* all there is!

ORRIN.   *(Out.)* I found her simple, sunny interpretations of the *Strategies* course ... irresistible!

GAIL.   *(Out.)* As the *Strategies* say, "Once you recognize your own power, life can be like the fabled horn of plenty. Ever yielding more fruit, a limitless supply." I've always believed that anyway!

ORRIN. *(Out.)* She really did!

GAIL. *(Out.)* I'm gonna work late again tonight! Then I'm gonna go home and study more!

ORRIN. *(Out.)* My transference ... was complete. I was determined not to repeat my fatal mistake with Stephanie: I would show up on *this* radar! *(Light change: Orrin and Gail sit on the roof, having lunch, looking out at the Manhattan skyline.)*

GAIL. I love rooftops! They're great!

ORRIN. I've been having lunch up here by myself for weeks.

GAIL. That midtown skyline is ... exquisite! Like big canyons! Square and pointy; pointy and square ...

ORRIN. The Chrysler Building's my favorite.

GAIL. Yes! It's breathtaking!

ORRIN. It actually has some wonderful gargoyles, when you go up there, and look closely.

GAIL. I must do that sometime.

ORRIN. I'll take you! If ... you want.

GAIL. What's that one down there? To the south?

ORRIN. The Municipal Building. Architecturally underrated, I think.

GAIL. It's magnificent! *(As Orrin talks, Gail stands, closes her eyes and opens her arms out to the city. This distracts him.)*

ORRIN. Yes, that gold plating is ... certainly unique, in a lot of ... ways ... and ... and ...

GAIL. It's the city of my dreams ...

ORRIN. Many people have thought that, yeah.

GAIL. The city which most shines for me.

ORRIN. Yeah, a lot of other people have thought that, historically speaking. Then they come here, too, from all over the place, and then — bam! The boot heel slams right down on their faces. Lots of —

GAIL. I mean that it *is* the city of my dreams, Orrin. Now, not in the past. A dream come *true.*

ORRIN. Really?

GAIL. Really.

ORRIN. Even with all the pushing, the noise, the hatred? The awful smells?

GAIL. That's just what comes when people are confused.

ORRIN. What are they so confused about?

GAIL. The riches here. The abundance of everything — of life!

ORRIN. That's ... true. *(He gulps hard, then dares to say.)* I like ... the way you think.

GAIL. I don't think too hard. I just ... move through each day.

ORRIN. Then I ... like the way you do that.

GAIL. Thank you. That's sweet, Orrin.

ORRIN. No, sorry ... I don't mean to say that I like *you,* so much as the way you have of thinking, or whatever? ... Or of, you know, as you say, of moving through each day, and —

GAIL. But you do ... like me, don't you?

ORRIN. Ummm. Yes. I do.

GAIL. I'm glad. Because I like you, very much.

ORRIN. Thank you.

GAIL. Your eyes are so gentle.

ORRIN. Seriously?

GAIL. And you always smell like baby shampoo.

ORRIN. Oh. I use it frequently. Every day, I guess, for ... scalp ... reasons ...

GAIL. And you're kind!

ORRIN. I am?

GAIL. Yes. I feel so lucky to have met the three of you! Russell and Stephanie, they're amazing! They've become my mentors!

ORRIN. Mine ... too.

GAIL. Stephanie is so beautiful! So strong! And Russell — what a — ! Wow!

ORRIN. What? Russell, what a what?

GAIL. What a mind, I guess I mean!

ORRIN. Yes. A big throbbing one.

GAIL. And then there's you!

ORRIN. There is?

GAIL. Yes! And you should know that your kindness counts in this world. A lot!

ORRIN. Thank you, Gail.

GAIL. You're a ... good person.

ORRIN. *(His smile fades. Miserably.)* Excuse me ... for asking, but was all that a nice-as-can-be way of saying: "Just friends, but no more?"

GAIL. Not ... necessarily.

ORRIN. *(He brightens again.)* Oh my GOD! That's — that's — ! The Present Moment Is All There Is, right?

GAIL. Yes! Isn't that great?

ORRIN. Yes! *(He rushes over to her, grabs her hand. Blurts out all at once.)* You smell like apricots, so suddenly I love apricots! You look at New York City, a place I think of only in the most apocalyptic of terms at this point, and I love it through your eyes, all over again! I love the air around you, the air around you is filled with stars and planets and buzzing satellites and ... really cool exotic purple birds! I don't know what the hell I'm saying. Just — You put your hand on something, and I love it! You set your beautiful eyes on anything, and it's new and wonderful again! The world is lucky to be gazed at by you! I love you. I love you! *(Pause. This hangs in the air for a moment.)*

GAIL. I ... like you a lot, too, Orrin.

ORRIN. Oh no ... Oh, God ...

GAIL. Ssshh, wait! ... I may not be ready to say "love" just yet, only 'cause that's too fast for me ...

ORRIN. Of course! God, what a pushy bastard I am!

GAIL. Stop, please! I'm very flattered.

ORRIN. Pushy, carpe diem, lover-boy asshole!

GAIL. Sssshh! Stop it! It makes me very happy, to hear you say you feel that way about me. I'm honored — from someone as nice as you?

ORRIN. Nice but ... pushy!

GAIL. Ssshhh. *(She takes his hand.)* Thank you.

ORRIN. Oh, God ...

GAIL. We have time, Orrin. Lots of rooftop lunches. *(She kisses him: a peck on the cheek.)* We have so much time. *(She smiles, walks away. He is overwhelmed with joy.)*

ORRIN. We do! We have ... time! *(Lights shift: the office. Stephanie on the phone, in high business mode. Russell and Gail watching, hovering expectantly.)*

STEPHANIE. *(On phone.)* Listen, we're gonna overnight that to you immediately, Don. If not sooner.

ORRIN. *(Out.)* But no stray minutes during the next few weeks. A sizable animation company in LA was suddenly interested in Little Russell. The partnership could make a bundle!

STEPHANIE. Right, Don. We have a very nice new series of little Russell scuba-diving … *(Laughs.)* That's right, Don! Cuter than hell!

ORRIN. *(Out.)* No one was allowed to talk to the company but Stephanie. Oddly, this was not her rule, but Russell's. *(Orrin joins the scene, watches Stephanie.)*

RUSSELL. 'Cause things are very delicate right now … And this woman knows how to work it, baby!

GAIL. Wow.

STEPHANIE. He's swimming around the Australian barrier reef … Right, Gail?

GAIL. Yes! Bermuda shorts, full gear! I also put some nice starfish in there, to —

STEPHANIE. Quiet. OK, Don. Thanks, honey. That goes right out, Pony Express. Ciao! *(She hangs up.)* Post Office run, Orrin!

RUSSELL. Well? Is he close?

STEPHANIE. He's close, Don's close, but he doesn't have the absolute final word. His boss needs something that sparks his imagination.

RUSSELL. I wish we could send his boss the *Strategies* tapes! God, why don't we? Yeah! We'll send him the tapes! That would be a bold move!

STEPHANIE. Don't be ridiculous.

RUSSELL. You know, Steph, just 'cause you've been lukewarm about *Strategies* lately, doesn't mean the three of us still aren't mining a lot of gold out of them. Maybe Don and his boss just need to do a few Imagination Slams, then —

STEPHANIE. They aren't looking for a new lifestyle! They want us to do some *work!*

RUSSELL. Sor-ry!

STEPHANIE. Fucking headache again. — He needs us to

49

sharpen things conceptually. Some angle that suggests a Saturday morning kids' series. But we do the work for him, get it?

RUSSELL.   A series! Jesus, that's the mother lode! That flowers into toys, and T-shirts, and Halloween costumes!

GAIL.   God! That's ... great!

RUSSELL.   Aren't you excited, Steph?

STEPHANIE.   It doesn't matter! Let's get to work! Orrin, get these ready, and go! Gail, crank out more cute little fuckers! Russell, make yourself useful ... I don't know, somehow. *Inspire* us ... Or whatever the hell you do here at this point.

RUSSELL.   What is your problem?

STEPHANIE.   Nothing! Just somebody else fucking DO something! It's like being in business with a bunch of kindergartners! This isn't Junior Achievement, boys and girls, this is Hollywood on the line! *(They get to work. Orrin stuffs envelopes as he talks.)*

ORRIN.   *(Out.)* Things had been tense between Russell and Stephanie for weeks, but I didn't want to know any more. I'd been avoiding Russell's oppressive confidences.

GAIL.   Wow. That's great, though!

ORRIN.   *(Out.)* Because things were hopeful with Gail — we were so busy, but we kept saying we'd have another rooftop lunch together soon. So we didn't need their toxic relationship contaminating ours!

GAIL.   Maybe little Russell as an expert in kickboxing ...

ORRIN.   *(Out.)* I loved her! She always bravely tried to dispel the tension.

GAIL.   Saturday morning cartoons! Wow! I used to be totally glued to them every weekend when I was a kid! My favorites were Scooby Doo and the Whacky Races!

ORRIN.   Me too! I liked the Whacky Races, too! I loved the Whacky Races!

GAIL.   Me too! And I drew a whole Saturday line-up of my own cartoon programs! I had it all planned out, from seven A.M. to noon! Including the commercials! Wow, isn't it great, Orrin? That that dream of mine may come true?

ORRIN.   Yes, Gail!

GAIL.   That we ourselves may actually be responsible for some-

thing a kid of today will love? And cherish? And remember for-
ever?

ORRIN.   Yes, Gail!

GAIL.   God, Orrin, I can't believe it! If it really happened! It's
hard to believe! I never would have guessed that when I first
sketched the little bugger on the napkin! It just took ten seconds! So I never thought — I — ummm. *(This hangs in the air.
Russell subtly shoots an alarmed look over to Gail. Stephanie finally
looks up.)*

STEPHANIE.   Pardon me?

RUSSELL.   You mean when you first copied it. Right?

GAIL.   Right. When I —

RUSSELL.   Right. When you —

STEPHANIE.   Shut up. What did you say, Gail? On the ... napkin?

GAIL.   No, I mean —

RUSSELL.   She means —

STEPHANIE.   God, I'm dense!

GAIL.   I mean ... copied it, Stephanie. *From* the napkin.

STEPHANIE.   Uh-uh. No. *(Strolls over to Gail, begins to crowd
her.)* No, Gail. Darling. I don't think you can do it.

GAIL.   What?

STEPHANIE.   I don't think — Gail, sweetie — that when I
come this close to your face ... And look you straight in the
eye ... And ask you if this fading little bunch of lines and squig-
gles on this greasy, dog-eared napkin, is an original work of
yours ... I don't think you can lie about it. *(Gail looks away,
scared.)* Effectively, anyway. It's not you.

GAIL.   I just ... copied it. Russell, he did the original.

STEPHANIE.   Gosh. No. No, I still don't think — Gail, darling, I'm still here — I still remain unconvinced that you can
sit there, with me looking in your eye — as you'll notice if you
dare to peek up, I'm still doing right now, and I'm not about
to stop, you perky, simpering little woman-child! — I don't
think you can tell me that this isn't your work.

GAIL.   It ... isn't ... *(She begins to cry.)*

STEPHANIE.   I'm still hovering over you, Gail. Two inches
from your face. Now, once again: Is this —

51

RUSSELL. *Yes,* OK? God, Stephanie, don't torture her! I fucked up, all right? Not her!

STEPHANIE. You drew this thing, and you'd let this wanker take the credit for it?

GAIL. It ... was the only way I ... got to work here ...

STEPHANIE. Do you like being a doormat, is that it?

GAIL. No!

STEPHANIE. You enjoy being a *tool?* Listen, you crybaby ... I made the same mistake last year. Worked for people who took me for granted, put limits on me 'cause I'm a woman —

RUSSELL. Yeah we've all heard the Legend of Stephanie's Last Stand before, OK? It's not like you were Gloria Steinem, Steph, you tried to steal other lawyer's clients! It's considered unethical!

STEPHANIE. Any man would have been congratulated for being aggressive! And who are you to talk ethics, about anything, you — !

RUSSELL. No, the real point is that you're mired in the past, and way bitter about it. And you're looking for a reason to get at me, because you continue to believe that all these ... assignations, with other women, are happening ... 'Cause you get a migraine or two ... *(Stephanie rushes over and begins to crowd him now, backing him up by repeatedly jabbing him in the chest with her finger.)*

STEPHANIE. You lied to me, you fucking asshole! And if you lied to me about this, then you can lie to me about anything!

RUSSELL. Steph, don't be paranoid ...

STEPHANIE. You're not the artful goddamned deceiver you think you are, Russell! But I tried to believe you. As hard as I could! And now I find out I'm a fool for even bothering! You do lie to me! And I cannot tolerate that shit, you smug fucking prick!

RUSSELL. Stop it, Steph! Please! Just stop —

STEPHANIE. You want me to stop? OK, I'll stop. *(Picks up her briefcase, makes for the door.)* Good-bye, boys and girls.

RUSSELL. Stephanie! *(Stephanie walks out, slams the door.)* Aw, please! Stephanie! *(Opens the door, runs after her. We hear his shouts as Orrin comes over to comfort Gail.)*

ORRIN. It's OK, Gail …

GAIL. She was mean.

RUSSELL. *(Off.)* Stephanie, don't be absurd!

ORRIN. She was mean to me once too.

RUSSELL. *(Off.)* Come on, Steph! I'm sorry, all right? Steph?

ORRIN. And I'm OK now. See?

RUSSELL. *(Off.)* Stephanie! Don't be a — oh, forget it. *(Russell reenters, briskly.)* She'll get over it. *(Spot on Orrin.)*

ORRIN. *(Out.)* But she did not. One day, two days, a week, two weeks: Stephanie did not return to the office. *(Lights shift: the office again, two weeks later. Russell hangs up the phone; Gail watches.)*

RUSSELL. She hasn't returned calls, or answered her doorbell either. So we have to assume that Stephanie is gone for good.

GAIL. Oh God, I'm sorry! It's my fault.

RUSSELL. It's mine. Forget it.

ORRIN. *(Out.)* I thought Russell was taking an uncharacteristic amount of responsibility.

RUSSELL. I'll be spearheading this operation for a while. I'm in charge.

ORRIN. *(Out.)* And I thought, "Yeah! It *is* better, for all of us, that Stephanie's gone." Russell was right: She may have been handling the business with skill, but that she was otherwise spinning out of control. With her out of the picture for keeps, everything seemed to be making itself right. And the *Strategies* seemed more powerful than ever! *(Orrin joins the scene. He watches Gail adoringly.)*

RUSSELL. I'm in charge. Everything goes through me from now on. And we're going back to basics. To the straight, undiluted *Strategies for Power* principles.

GAIL. Great!

ORRIN. Great!

GAIL. That way things will be more positive!

RUSSELL. Exactly!

ORRIN. Exactly!

GAIL. Great! *(Russell dials the phone.)* I felt like I was getting thrown out of the present moment again and again, over the last few weeks! It started to actually, physically hurt!

RUSSELL. Yes! — Hello, Don Greenberg please. Russell Boam calling from New York.

GAIL. And you know how they say in *Strategies* about your horizons being unlimited, Orrin? Well, I started to feel mine becoming limited! Really limited!

ORRIN. And they're not! Isn't it wonderful?

GAIL. It is, Orrin! Oh, my heart just aches when I think of the doors I shut on myself!

ORRIN. Me too!

RUSSELL. — Don! Russell Boam. I'm Stephanie Rommell's partner ... Steph has had a touch of the flu ... Yeah, and it looks like she'll be bedridden for a while longer ...

GAIL. But no limits!

RUSSELL. Five or six weeks, tops ...

GAIL. No boundaries!

RUSSELL. — No, she's fine! But I'm gonna have to take up the ball for a while.

GAIL. None at all!

RUSSELL. — Oh! The ball? ... "Take up the ball" ... as in: You'll be conducting business with me for a while.

GAIL. Skies that never end. Wow! *(Spot on Orrin.)*

ORRIN. *(Out.)* Everything seemed fresh and new again! We rhapsodized about the latest *Strategies* tapes. I was eager to show what a valuable member of this new team I was — so I stayed late one night, casting more bread on the water: faxing out a whole new round of promotional teasers across the country. I was exhausted by ten o'clock, with a few more hours of work to go. As per my secret guilty habit, I crawled underneath my desk for a short nap. *(He does so.)* I had a bizarre nightmare: little Russell, marching through the pages of humanity's recorded time. Little Russell was distorted. Huge. A fanged, bloody-eyed, half-human, half-beast, at the command of a tremendous army of like creatures, hell-bent on conquering the world. They trudged through every continent, trampling villages and then whole cities; through each year, each century, grabbing and looting. Grabbing what they needed and what they did not, just for the thrill of acquisition. Through Ancient Sumeria, through pharonic Egypt, through Shungan dynasty

India, through Hannibal's Carthage and through Rome of the Caesars, fast-forwarding up through Medieval Spain, through Elizabethan England and Ancien Regime France, through Imperial Japan and Peronista Argentina, and concluding with a final march across our United States, their numbers swelled so that they could easily sweep from the Atlantic to the Pacific in hundred-deep columns, lined north to south — starting at Times Square then pushing, pushing west, pushing, and finally winding up on Sunset Boulevard, the enormous army camped victoriously, gorging themselves with all the Fatburgers they could stuff down their gullets ... The giant, bloated Ur-Russell, his cute fuzz now matted with gore, Giant Little Russell, dictator of the world, enthroned above it all, booming: "It's all mine! More, more, more! Now, now, now! MORE!" I was comforted to be woken up by the familiar sound of our office door opening. *(It opens. Russell enters, looks around.)*

RUSSELL.   Hello? Orrin? Orrin? Hello? *(Russell darts back out the door as Orrin begins to get out from under the desk, sheepishly. He quickly retreats and freezes when he sees Russell reentering carrying Gail. Her arms and legs are wrapped tight around him; in a hungry kiss. Finally they come up for air.)*

GAIL.   It just feels weird, always doing it here. It reminds me of ... things, here at work. *(Russell gets right to work undressing.)*

RUSSELL.   I'm on someone's couch these days, you have about fifty roommates — where else do we have?

GAIL.   I know ...

RUSSELL.   Any port in a storm, you know?

GAIL.   You're right. *(Russell takes a condom out of shirt pocket, hands it to Gail, then whips off his shirt. They kiss hungrily. Finally, Gail pulls away, gently.)*

GAIL.   But Russell. Something's weighing on my conscience.

RUSSELL.   A "conscience." You know from the tapes what a relative value that is ... Our old-brain conditioning. It's really guilt, and guilt is absolutely useless. *(He takes off his pants.)*

GAIL.   I know, but —

RUSSELL.   But nothing ... Remember what it said: "Carrying guilt about anything is like trying to walk through the world shrink-wrapped in plastic." 100% true!

GAIL.   I know, but — I'm afraid I've hurt someone.
RUSSELL.   Who?
ORRIN.   *(Out.)* Me! Surely it was me!
GAIL.   It's ... you.
RUSSELL.   Me?
ORRIN.   *(Out.)* Him?
GAIL.   Yes! When I was talking to Orrin —
ORRIN.   *(Out.)* Yes! Please, at least that!
GAIL.   When I told Orrin a couple of weeks ago, about the ... napkin? When it slipped out?
RUSSELL.   *(More interested now.)* Yeah?
GAIL.   I ... meant it to slip out.
RUSSELL.   *(Shocked.)* You ... you backstabber!
GAIL.   I'm sorry!
RUSSELL.   You little ... sneak! It was possibly forgivable if you did it 'cause of a memory lapse, but to consciously break our agreement — !
GAIL.   I know. I'm sorry!
RUSSELL.   You put everything in jeopardy! You ... saboteur!
GAIL.   I'm sorry, I'm sorry! But it — wasn't fair!
RUSSELL.   Wasn't fair?
GAIL.   It was the tapes! They said assert yourself in the world, re-shape your Interpersonal Ecosystem to fit you, rather than the reverse. Sequence Twelve: "The World as Your Mirror!"
RUSSELL.   I know, but — shit!
GAIL.   ... And I drew him, and you three were partners, and you were going to make a ton of money from this deal, but I drew him, and — it wasn't fair! I agree with what Stephanie said, even if she was really mean! When things just aren't fair, you just have to — ! *(Russell begins to laugh: a chuckle at first, then bigger.)* What's so funny?
RUSSELL.   You! *(He kisses her.)* You're wonderful!
GAIL.   I am?
RUSSELL.   You are, you're — phenomenal! And you're right. It could be more fair.
GAIL.   Really? So?
RUSSELL.   But we're stuck with this arrangement. Me a partner; Orrin a partner; and you the employee.

GAIL. No we're not stuck with it. You could talk to Orrin. I'm sure he'd agree.

RUSSELL. What if I don't want to share with another partner? This LA thing may yet come through. And a two-way split is healthier than a three-way.

GAIL. You don't want to share?

RUSSELL. What if, I said? Hypothetically?

GAIL. Then I'd ... I'd quit. And there'd be no one to do Russell. Do little Russell, I mean. *Draw.*

RUSSELL. Hmm. You'd quit. Hmm.

GAIL. I'm very sorry. I am trying to be true to the spirit of Sequence Twelve.

RUSSELL. You're really starting to turn me on.

GAIL. What do you say, though?

RUSSELL. I say you're turning me way, way ON. You're giving me more of a fight than I ever, ever bargained for ... And that gets me all weak-kneed!

GAIL. And — ?

RUSSELL. And you win. I'll talk to Orrin during our morning Productivity Slam. You're right, he won't be a problem. I think he has the hots for you.

GAIL. I know. It was cute when it started; now it makes me a little sad.

RUSSELL. And I should thank you! 'Cause you've reminded me of some basics here. I'd forgotten my Sequence Seventeen. "Pruning Your Tree." In order to grow, we need what's essential, and no more, at this critical time. We need to cut back.

GAIL. What do you mean?

RUSSELL. I mean I'm still not thrilled with our number going up to three partners again. And I want to respect the truth of that strong feeling I have. Honor it with unequivocating action.

GAIL. *(Pulling back, warily.)* But you said you'd make me a partner!

RUSSELL. And I will. You're essential; you've called my hand on that. You are a branch that cannot be pruned. But —

GAIL. Russell, no ...

RUSSELL. ... But do we really need a partner who's just a glorified mail-boy?

GAIL. Oh, Russell! No, no! That's … awful!

RUSSELL. That's your Old Brain again. He's not happy here anyway! I know him, he's my best friend! It's nothing he ever wanted to do. And he never really mastered the *Strategies*. Philosophically, we had to float his ass for the longest time. So —

GAIL. God! That's — that just gives me the shivers!

RUSSELL. Here, I'll warm you. *(He pulls her in close; lifts her up again. She gratefully wraps herself around him.)* You're shivering because you're growing. It's scary; it makes all your physical and physiological systems tremble, these quantum jumps forward …

GAIL. Poor Orrin …

RUSSELL. We'll do it once you're a partner. We'll do it gracefully; and we'll do it with the spirit of charity which he has definitely earned. Though preferably before LA comes through. But it will all be a gift to him, in the long run — we'll be affording him a rich life lesson.

GAIL. I … guess … That's true …

RUSSELL. Of course it is.

GAIL. I guess so. I … I have to expand my thinking more …

RUSSELL. I'll help you.

GAIL. Will you?

RUSSELL. *(As he speaks, he walks them over to the desk under which Orrin hides. Places her down.)* We're the vanguard, Gail. This New Brain thinking is an inevitable force; a hurricane that's coming, like it or not. The academics and the politicians are just beginning to catch on; just starting to surf this wave. And we're way out in front of them all! *(He crawls up on it with her, begins kissing her neck. She begins unbuttoning.)*

GAIL. But there's time to learn, isn't there? There's lots of time?

RUSSELL. There's no time. None at all. There's right now, and that's all there is. And I'm here with you, right now, wanting to love you.

GAIL. Great! *(She pulls him down to her, with surprising strength. They kiss passionately. Orrin quietly leaves his place under the desk.*

58

He's leaving "theatrically" — not in the room with Russell and Gail.
He produces a big bottle.)

ORRIN.   *(Out.)* After they finally left — three and a half noisy hours later — I ran out and got this bottle of mead. I'm not a drinker. I just remembered it from the Beowulf saga. Between battles with the monster Grendel, Beowulf and the other Vikings used to drink this stuff. It's a honey liqueur. I walked around the city all night, chugging it, asking myself: What Do I Want? What I Wanted was to give over to my rage; with blood in my eyes. After all, even the most revered of the ancient leaders were given to occasional baseness. David had Bathsheeba's husband killed: a major lapse of niceness indeed. And one impulse could be too tempting for even the greatest philosopher-kings. That is: *revenge.* To open the cage, let your lions loose; let them rampage. But I was shy; I never even let myself get publicly annoyed, much less enraged. I never had; and I knew I could not; and I knew I would not. So it was nearly morning when I remembered the time-honored Arabic proverb: "The enemy of my enemy is my friend." Dawn was breaking ...
(Lights up on office. The next morning: Russell and Gail wait.)
RUSSELL.   Where is he? Most of the time he's obscenely prompt. — Good morning, Don Greenberg, please? Russell Boam, in New York.
GAIL.   I'm scared.
RUSSELL.   Don't be. This is just phase one: I ask him to make you a partner. A cinch.
GAIL.   And I deserve it, right?
RUSSELL.   You sure do. — Yes? Ma'am, I've left a truly stunning number of messages for him over the last hour.
GAIL.   I *do* deserve it.
RUSSELL.   — No, ma'am, I'd rather not "take the hint," I'd rather speak with him directly. We've been checking in every morning for the last two weeks, then suddenly he can't take my call? I think — Hello? Hello! Rude old hag! *(Enter Orrin. He looks horrible: unkempt, exhausted, and dazed.)*
GAIL.   Hi, Orrin!
RUSSELL.   Orrin! Buddy! Our Productivity Slam was scheduled to start a half-hour ago!

59

ORRIN.   I am sorry to be so inconsiderate.

RUSSELL.   Well. No biggie.

ORRIN.   I am sorry and I am grateful for your magnanimity.

RUSSELL.   Huh?

GAIL.   Are you feeling all right, Orrin? You look … lopsided.

ORRIN.   I am sorry that I look lopsided.

GAIL.   Kind of flipped out.

ORRIN.   I am sorry that I look kind of flipped out.

RUSSELL.   You look ravishing. Here, sit down, Orrin, please. I have a little proposal I'd like to run by you. I'm sure you'll it find eminently fair and workable.

ORRIN.   If it's from you, Russell, I'm certain that it will be.

RUSSELL.   *(Pause.)* Was that a dig?

GAIL.   Orrin?

ORRIN.   No. I'm sorry. That was … not a dig.

RUSSELL.   Hm. Sounded like a dig.

GAIL.   It did, Orrin.

RUSSELL.   Well … don't worry about it. Now: What do you think of the idea of making Gail a partner here?

ORRIN.   I … Boy, I never expected that.

RUSSELL.   It's a superb idea, huh? So?

GAIL.   Orrin?

ORRIN.   Um, I think perhaps the … threshold question, here, is, you know: What Does Gail Want?

RUSSELL.   You feeling OK, buddy?

ORRIN.   Do you … desire, this, Gail?

GAIL.   God, I don't know — Russell suggested it, and I was really flattered! I guess it would be … nice.

ORRIN.   Hm.

GAIL.   It might even be … great!

ORRIN.   How about if it turns out — you know — awful? All of this, just awful?

RUSSELL.   That's a pretty grim forecast, Orrin. Really, bud!

GAIL.   Yes, Orrin. I'm much more optimistic about our future here! So — this is kinda embarrassing, but — I guess I do want it, yes!

ORRIN.   Well, I should really think about it.

GAIL.   Don't you want me to join you? Orrin?

RUSSELL. Come on, Orrin! Chop chop, now! Yes or no? Five Second Rule. Gail? One ...

GAIL. Two ...

RUSSELL. Three ...

GAIL. Four ...

ORRIN. OK. Sure. Yes.

GAIL. Wow! Thanks, Orrin!

ORRIN. Yes, but ...

RUSSELL. Excellent! So Gail's the third partner! Now! Here's our battle plan for today ...

ORRIN. But I think your count is off by one, Russell.

RUSSELL. What?

ORRIN. I mean, I think we should check with all the partners first. *(Enter Stephanie, briefcase in hand. She looks fresh as a daisy: impeccably dressed, all sunny smiles.)*

GAIL. Wow! Great!

RUSSELL. Jesus Christ ...

STEPHANIE. Yes, it is I. And I am risen.

GAIL. Hi Stephanie! Wow! Great! It's great to see you! Wow!

STEPHANIE. Hi honey. Russell?

RUSSELL. Steph.

STEPHANIE. Russell, am I to understand that I am no longer a partner here?

RUSSELL. Well, you just bolted! You don't return calls! What are we supposed to think?

STEPHANIE. Gosh, I just took a few days off, honey.

RUSSELL. A month!

STEPHANIE. Yes, and now I'm rested, refreshed, and ready to rock! Well! What's on our agenda for today? Orrin? Want to bring me up to speed?

ORRIN. Oh! Um, Russell ... Russell, he made a proposal that Gail should be a partner.

STEPHANIE. Interesting. Interesting.

GAIL. Just ... just out of fairness, Stephanie.

STEPHANIE. Interesting. Interesting. Not entirely unappealing, either.

GAIL. Really?

STEPHANIE. 'Fraid not, though. Nope. What's next?

RUSSELL. You can't just come in here and veto it! You left! The business would have died if not for us! Us *three!*

STEPHANIE. Business?

RUSSELL. Enterprise.

STEPHANIE. But that's what has me perplexed, Russell — what "business" is it that you've kept alive, precisely? How's the LA deal going?

RUSSELL. It's — well, it's had its shaky moments, but —

STEPHANIE. It's *dead,* dummy. You won't even get your calls returned starting today.

RUSSELL. How do you know?

STEPHANIE. I phoned Don Greenberg early this morning. Told him the partnership had suffered a schism, and that everything was on ice; and that I'd call him when and if things got going again. In the meantime, he could ignore calls from you. He was fine with that. He was getting a bit tired of your babble on the phone. "Tedious," I believe he called it.

RUSSELL. Steph, that's really not fair at all …

STEPHANIE. Shut up, Russell. Now kids: I come bearing a wee proposal of my own. Gail. Gail, how've you been, dear?

GAIL. Please … don't be mean to me again.

STEPHANIE. Of course not, honey. But you want to be a partner here? That's your ambition, dear?

GAIL. I … guess I don't have to be.

STEPHANIE. Oh, you won't be, I guarantee. But here's what the actual partnership would like to offer you in its stead: a contract giving you a very generous flat fee — the sum of $10,000.00, or 1% of the first year's gross earnings, whichever is greater — when and if the cartoon character currently known as "little Russell" — we must reconsider that name — ever becomes a commercially viable entity.

RUSSELL. Stephanie, what are you up to?

STEPHANIE. This contract, when signed, will be legally binding. It will also constitute your termination from this employ.

GAIL. You're trying to … get rid of me?

STEPHANIE. Not trying, sweetie. Doing.

GAIL. But you … need me!

STEPHANIE. Don't overestimate your star quality, dear. We'll just recruit some dreamy-eyed young artiste from … oh, Parsons. I imagine. If any money rolls in, our severance package will compensate you very fairly for your little … napkin. Any other artwork was done as a salaried employee of this partnership.

GAIL. I don't think I can sign that.

STEPHANIE. Do you need a pen?

GAIL. I don't think I … want to …

RUSSELL. Exactly! Don't sign it, Gail! Steph, really — you have no right — ! Gail, she has no legal right to —

STEPHANIE. Gail. Gail, honey, do you want to trust Russell's knowledge of the law? Or mine?

RUSSELL. She's trying to bully you, Gail. Be strong. Remember Sequence Twelve! Your Interpersonal Ecosystem! The World *Is* Your Mirror! It is!

GAIL. Oh, God — I don't know — Orrin! *(She rushes over to him, takes his hand.)* Orrin? Do you think what she's doing is fair?

ORRIN. Probably.

RUSSELL. What are you talking about? Orrin? Buddy?

ORRIN. Just that this might afford Gail a … rich life lesson.

GAIL. Oh.

RUSSELL. Oh.

GAIL. You know…?

ORRIN. As much as I care to.

GAIL. So … I guess I shouldn't count on you to — ?

ORRIN. Oh, I think … not. *(Gives Gail her hand back.)*

STEPHANIE. Gail? The numbers simply aren't going your way. So let's not take all day, sweetie.

RUSSELL. Don't, Gail! We'll make it happen together! You and me!

GAIL. But Russell, she's … scaring me!

STEPHANIE. Good.

RUSSELL. If you do sign, we'll have a very hard time moving forward in our relationship, OK?

STEPHANIE. Gail? Honey? Your choice. The indefinite companionship of Mr. Studmuffins, here, or …

RUSSELL. I mean it, Gail!

STEPHANIE. Or ... some profit.

RUSSELL. I'll have to consider the possibility that you really don't care about me!

STEPHANIE. Gail?

GAIL. I'll ... God, I — ! Ten thousand?

STEPHANIE. Yup.

GAIL. Make it fifteen.

STEPHANIE. That's do-able. Here. I'll change it, initial it. *(She makes an adjustment on the contract.)* Now what do you say, dear? Man or money? Five second rule: One ... Two ... Three ...

ORRIN. Four ...

GAIL. *(Chillier now.)* I'll take the fucking cash.

STEPHANIE. A stellar choice. *(Gail signs.)*

GAIL. You people are a bunch of goddamned freaks!

STEPHANIE. Your copy. *(Gail takes it, goes to the door. Turns.)*

GAIL. *(Bitterly.)* It's always the artist who gets screwed. *(She exits.)*

RUSSELL. You're a terrorist, Stephanie! That was just ... un-called for!

STEPHANIE. As for you. Mr. Russell Boam. I think —

RUSSELL. But all right! Good! Very funny, very nice. You zinged me, Steph. I definitely had it coming. — She really gave me a schooling there, didn't she, buddy? OK. But now let's take a deep breath here for a second, look for a Conjunction, and start some serious Bridge-building, before things go too far, and —

STEPHANIE. We're speaking a different language right now, honey. Mr. Russell Boam. The partnership will now entertain a motion to ... dis-include you.

RUSSELL. Stephanie. Come on. You don't want to do that.

STEPHANIE. *Au contraire.*

RUSSELL. Well, you *can't* do that! OK?

STEPHANIE. Beg to differ. I can. *We* can.

RUSSELL. Orrin! Orrin, buddy! I know I'm a highly flawed human being. But we've been friends for how long, now? You want to exile me just for ... stumbling a bit?

ORRIN. It's ... how I'm wired, I guess.

64

STEPHANIE. Orrin is in fact the real player here. See, when he dropped over at five A.M. this morning, my first instinct was to throw him down the stairs ...

ORRIN. I knew she didn't like me. But I —

STEPHANIE. It's not that. You were always just too goddamn busy adoring me to even take seriously.

ORRIN. Right.

STEPHANIE. ... And frankly, I didn't want to see *any* of you, ever again. But he was so ... pathetic, and he smelled like this horrible ... fermented honey ...

ORRIN. Mead ...

STEPHANIE. So I listened to his tale of woe. About your private little Imagination Slam with Miss Chirpy Chipmunk, here. I mean, Russell, it was bad enough that you two were rutting in the office — but then when he told me you were going to try and grab everything we worked for here — ! That I could not tolerate!

ORRIN. I can't tolerate ... anything ...

STEPHANIE. And when he showed me this ...

ORRIN. My receipt. I always get a receipt.

STEPHANIE. ... I was reminded that legally, he's always been the de facto owner of this enterprise, whatever it constitutes, being as he remains its sole investor.

ORRIN. Paper route money ...

STEPHANIE. He is de facto chairman of the board. This overrides any ad hoc structure of partnership. So, Mr. Chairman?

ORRIN. *(To Russell.)* You're ... fired.

RUSSELL. I could take you to court.

STEPHANIE. Mr. Orrin Hoover has granted me power of attorney.

ORRIN. That's true.

STEPHANIE. And I would greatly relish playing this out in the legal arena with you, Mr. Boam. Until then, you will kindly clear the premises.

RUSSELL. Guys! Stop this! You're talking like fucking pod people! It's giving me the chills!

ORRIN. Maybe you're growing.

RUSSELL. Huh?

STEPHANIE. I talked to security downstairs about this when I came in. Two extremely large ex-convicts; and they like me a lot. They're ready to come right up if I give them a jingle.

RUSSELL. Steph ...

STEPHANIE. Please clear out your things immediately.

RUSSELL. *(Long pause.)* Well. Well then. Looks like I'm ... gone.

STEPHANIE. Clever boy. *(Silence as he gathers his things, then.)*

RUSSELL. You know what? You're right. You're both right. I've been living a very ... sloppy life. And I apologize for the hurt I've caused you both. *(Pause as he gathers more of his stuff.)* And much as it wounds to be on the receiving end, I just have to say this to both of you: *(Smiles.)* That was phenomenal! Really, my compliments! You just — God! — you both just did a masterful job of applying the *Strategies:* relentlessly, bearing down, with complete faith. Steph, honey, you've really kept yourself sharp this past month. That vocabulary shift you did on me, back into legalese? Brilliant! You knew it would intimidate the shit out of me, and it did. And Orrin! ... I underestimated your commitment to the key basics. You were *cold,* my friend. You were *ice.* You should be proud, buddy. You guys are true warriors! And ... and while I know it might be hard to make room for this now, I still consider you both my friends. Stephanie, you're a remarkable woman, and — I'm truly sorry, but — I'm still in love with you.

STEPHANIE. Then why did you go mess it up?

RUSSELL. I wish I knew. I do. I know I will know someday. I'm 100% sure I will. So ... God, this is hard, but ... If you could find it, somehow, someday, in your heart, to forgive me, then maybe someday — I don't know — *(Pause. Stephanie is silent.)* Down the road somewhere ... *(Stephanie is silent. She seems to be softening.)* Or even ... soon, if you can find the space within you to —

STEPHANIE. Russell ...

RUSSELL. If only ... *(He shrugs, smiles.)* You too, Orrin, if you could ever find a way to let me back into — *(Orrin springs to his feet, surprising everyone, including himself. He slowly advances on him menacingly.)*

ORRIN.   DIE! DIE, CAESAR! DIE, NAPOLEON! ROT ON THE ISLAND OF ELBA! WE BANISH YOU, WE SOW SALT IN YOUR FIELDS! *(Russell backs off, a bit spooked. Their lines overlap.)*

RUSSELL.   What?

ORRIN.   ... DIE THE DEATH OF A MANGY DOG! MACHIA-VELLI! DIE, USURPER! TYRANT!

RUSSELL.   Orrin, I never took anything that wasn't freely given to me!

ORRIN.   ... DIE, MOUNTEBANK! CUCKOLDER! DISSEM-BLER! DIE, DIE, DIE! FOR CHRIST'S SAKE, CAN'T I EVEN GET A DECENT BIT OF REVENGE? DIE! *(Orrin stands glaring, breathing heavily.)*

RUSSELL.   I'm ... I'm sorry you feel that way, buddy. *(Piles the huge stack of* Strategies for Power *tapes and books into his arms.)* You don't mind if I take these? *(Russell's at the door. He stops; smiles.)* Weird. I don't think I've ever felt closer to you two. *(Russell exits. Orrin shouts after him.)*

ORRIN.   BASTARD! *(He walks back into the room like a trauma victim. He and Stephanie stare ahead in stunned silence for a moment. Then Orrin reanimates, begins pacing, ranting.)* ... Goddamnit, he ruins everything! He took my money, he took my self-respect, he took Gail, then he took my revenge!

STEPHANIE.   *(Disgusted.)* Shit, you really liked that little child-woman, didn't you?

ORRIN.   Yes! Loved her!

STEPHANIE.   Oh? ... More than you loved me?

ORRIN.   No! Yes! No! I don't know ...

STEPHANIE.   Jesus, it's pathetic! You give yourself away to people so ... abruptly!

ORRIN.   I guess.

STEPHANIE.   I always thought your real crush was on Russell, anyway.

ORRIN.   Maybe.

STEPHANIE.   You should look into that.

ORRIN.   Maybe. I don't know anything.

STEPHANIE.   *(Starting to really light into him.)* You can't just throw yourself at anyone that pats you on the head! Can't hide your intelligence, just because it's safer! You do that, you know!

It makes me sick to watch it!

ORRIN. Hey! Hey, wait a minute! You know? You know, you shouldn't talk, you know!

STEPHANIE. What!

ORRIN. You jumped in pretty quick, too, you know! You know? With him, and then those fucking tapes! And just now! Just now you looked like you were ready to stroll off to the junior prom with him, just 'cause he said a few goopey words to you!

STEPHANIE. What bullshit! At least I'm not as bad as *you!* At least I don't — ! I never — ! *(Pause.)* I mean, you can't compare the way — ! *(Pause.)* At least I didn't — ! *(Pause. She sighs.)* Oh ... forget it. You're right. What a loser I am. *(Pause.)* This whole year has been a big car crash. *(Pause.)* Getting fired. Then ... Russell. And the *Strategies* ... *(Pause.)* I always have higher hopes than I let myself admit. *(Pause.)* What a loser.

ORRIN. Don't say that.

STEPHANIE. A complete loser.

ORRIN. You're *not*. *(Pause.)* Anyway, I should thank you.

STEPHANIE. For what?

ORRIN. Coming here. I don't know what I would have done if you didn't —

STEPHANIE. Ssshh, ssshh. *(Pause.)* I had my own slimy reasons.

ORRIN. But still ... You helped me, and —

STEPHANIE. Sssh, please, honey. Don't embarrass me. *(Long pause. They stare out: accident victims.)*

ORRIN. Ummm. *(Cautiously.)* Do you ... want to keep this going?

STEPHANIE. What?

ORRIN. The office?

STEPHANIE. You're kidding.

ORRIN. No.

STEPHANIE. *(Pause.)* The lovable critter?

ORRIN. Yes.

STEPHANIE. Well ... I don't know. What do you want to do?

ORRIN. I don't know. Give it a ... try?

STEPHANIE. Well ...

ORRIN.   I promise I won't ... stare at you.

STEPHANIE.   *(Pause. With dead seriousness.)* Deal. *(They shake hands, businesslike. Quick light shift: spot on Orrin.)*

ORRIN.   *(Out.)* Back to Ancient Greece for just one second: As I said, when the Athenians asked Solon to take the job of Tyrant, he politely declined. Instead of grabbing all that power, he bought himself a ship and went into a voluntary exile for ten years. Just seeing the word, seeking wisdom! And — in my opinion — having a well-deserved, party-down, vacation. In his own chronicles of this ten-year trip, the most bombastic thing one can find is this — writing about himself in the third person, this is: "Each day he grew older and learned something new." He knew that true wisdom is mostly acquired the hard way ... For example ... *(Stephanie steps into the light, joins Orrin in his direct narration to the audience.)*

STEPHANIE.   *(Out.)* Everything *seemed* to work out well, for all four of us ... *(Gail suddenly appears in a spotlight.)*

ORRIN.   *(Out.)* Gail started a comic strip which had a meteoric rise to success, going into syndication all across the country ...

STEPHANIE.   *(Out.)* It was about a single working gal in the big city ...

GAIL.   *(Out.)* Her name is "Katie"! She has problems at her office job, and she always struggles with her weight — she loves chocolate cheesecake! — and her boyfriend Melvin has commitment problems. But she's basically real upbeat, and the strip is real real positive! *(Lights off Gail. Now Russell appears in a spotlight.)*

ORRIN.   *(Out.)* Russell became a regional director of *Strategies for Power* ...

STEPHANIE.   *(Out.)* And his star rose when they started holding huge seminars in the major cities ...

RUSSELL.   *(Out.)* They said we couldn't fill Madison Square Garden, but we did! I spoke in front of thousands of people, and left 'em wanting more!

STEPHANIE.   *(Out.)* But ...

RUSSELL.   *(Out.)* But I'm feeling a bit claustrophobic within the limits of the *Strategies* vocabulary. So I'm starting my own system of thinking! It's going to be big! Gigantic! *(Lights off Russell.)*

ORRIN. *(Out.)* But as for us ...

STEPHANIE. *(Out.)* Well, things were looking up for a while.

ORRIN. *(Out.)* I thought up a modest but workable angle to jump-start the animation deal. Stephanie worked out the particulars ...

STEPHANIE. *(Out.)* Educational TV! Our little fuzzy creature, Orrin the Otter ...

ORRIN. *(Out.)* We tried Orrin the Orangutan ...

STEPHANIE. *(Out.)* And Orrin the Oppossum ...

ORRIN. *(Out.)* Before making him an Otter. Even though his resemblance to a true otter was questionable.

STEPHANIE. *(Out.)* Orrin the Otter time-travelled through history, discovering all about what's come before ...

ORRIN. *(Out.)* He got into all sorts of scrapes ...

STEPHANIE. *(Out.)* But remained completely unfazed and serene despite everything.

ORRIN. *(Out.)* However, Orrin the Otter apparently did not charm the children of America.

STEPHANIE. *(Out.)* Or at least the critics. According to one, Orrin the Otter was ...

ORRIN. *(Out.)* "A detached, joyless little weasel whose adventures are clearly designed to proselytize an academic-liberal cant about the alleged lessons of history ..."

STEPHANIE. *(Out.)* Orrin the Otter was cited by one congressman as a reason to cut public TV funding ... Everyone panicked; the whole thing went belly up.

ORRIN. *(Out.)* We were able to pay off the original artist — who hardly needed the money at that point — and her art-school replacement ...

STEPHANIE. *(Out.)* Who never had the right touch anyway ... Kept trying to "post-modernize" the little fucker ...

ORRIN. *(Out.)* But beyond that, barely met our expenses. So: back to square one.

STEPHANIE. *(Out.)* Nothing. Nothing at all.

ORRIN. *(To Stephanie, a bit more privately.)* Except...?

STEPHANIE. What?

ORRIN.   A new ... friendship?

STEPHANIE.   Well ... I guess.

ORRIN.   *(Out. Back to audience, bubbling over.)* Yes, the true reward: a rich new friendship in the classical platonic mode! One in which loyalty and honesty are synonymous! One which, like that of Gilgamesh and Enkidu, will endure though every turn of life, and — !

STEPHANIE.   Honey?

ORRIN.   Yes?

STEPHANIE.   Relax.

ORRIN.   Right.

STEPHANIE.   We have time.

ORRIN.   Yeah.

STEPHANIE.   Plenty of time.

ORRIN.   Right. *(Music up: Lights fade to black.)*

THE END

PERFORMANCE NOTES

This is based on the experience of a few productions:

Much of this play should *fly,* though some scenes are meant to contrast this pace. In these, time should really be taken.

There seem to be a few traps for each character, which when avoided give the play a bit more depth *and* humor. In general, a less sentimental approach to the play works best.

It may seem necessary for ORRIN to be lovable to the audience, but consciously striving for that may have the opposite effect. If he's driven more simply by the intense need to tell the story to the audience, he will take us through the play better.

STEPHANIE should truly be the biggest dog on the block, wielding a fearsome authority when she wants. Though ultimately we learn that there are other dimensions to her, these shouldn't be telegraphed too early. She and RUSSELL should ooze sexuality together.

And though RUSSELL clearly has a big moral blind spot, he must be charming, sexy, and engaging enough — and sufficiently capable of showing true affection towards the others — for someone like STEPHANIE to take him seriously.

Lastly, GAIL should radiate innocent, even goofy, optimism almost until the bitter end — the less her turnaround is previewed, the better.

PROPERTY LIST

Paper bag (ORRIN) with:
    mineral water
Package (GAIL) with:
    books
    tapes
Piece of paper (STEPHANIE)
Walkman (STEPHANIE, RUSSELL)
Napkin and pen (RUSSELL)
Wallet with picture (RUSSELL)
Condom (RUSSELL)
Paper and pen (GAIL)
Lunch (ORRIN, GAIL)
Envelopes (ORRIN)
Briefcase (STEPHANIE)

NEW PLAYS

• **SMASH by Jeffrey Hatcher.** Based on the novel, AN UNSOCIAL SOCIALIST by George Bernard Shaw, the story centers on a millionaire Socialist who leaves his bride on their wedding day because he fears his passion for her will get in the way of his plans to overthrow the British government. *"SMASH is witty, cunning, intelligent, and skillful."* –Seattle Weekly. *"SMASH is a wonderfully high-style British comedy of manners that evokes the world of Shaw's high-minded heroes and heroines, but shaped by a post modern sensibility."* –Seattle Herald. [5M, 5W] ISBN: 0-8222-1553-5

• **PRIVATE EYES by Steven Dietz.** A comedy of suspicion in which nothing is ever quite what it seems. *"Steven Dietz's ... Pirandellian smooch to the mercurial nature of theatrical illusion and romantic truth, Dietz's spiraling structure and breathless pacing provide enough of an oxygen rush to revive any moribund audience member ... Dietz's mastery of playmaking ... is cause for kudos."* –The Village Voice. *"The cleverest and most artful piece presented at the 21st annual [Humana] festival was PRIVATE EYES by writer-director Steven Dietz."* –The Chicago Tribune. [3M, 2W] ISBN: 0-8222-1619-1

• **DIMLY PERCEIVED THREATS TO THE SYSTEM by Jon Klein.** Reality and fantasy overlap with hilarious results as this unforgettable family attempts to survive the nineties. *"Here's a play whose point about fractured families goes to the heart, mind -- and ears."* –The Washington Post. *" ... an end-of-the millennium comedy about a family on the verge of a nervous breakdown ... Trenchant and hilarious ... "* –The Baltimore Sun. [2M, 4W] ISBN: 0-8222-1677-9

• **HONOUR by Joanna Murray-Smith.** In a series of intense confrontations, a wife, husband, lover and daughter negotiate the forces of passion, lust, history, responsibility and honour. *"Tight, crackling dialogue (usually played out in punchy verbal duels) captures characters unable to deal with emotions ... Murray-Smith effectively places her characters in situations that strip away pretense."* –Variety. *"HONOUR might just capture a few honors of its own."* –Time Out Magazine. [1M, 3W] ISBN: 0-8222-1683-3

• **NINE ARMENIANS by Leslie Ayvazian.** A revealing portrait of three generations of an Armenian-American family. *" ... Ayvazian's obvious personal exploration ... is evocative, and her picture of an American Life colored nostalgically by an increasingly alien ethnic tradition, is persuasively embedded into a script of a certain supple grace ... "* –The NY Post. *"... NINE ARMENIANS is a warm, likable work that benefits from ... Ayvazian's clear-headed insight into the dynamics of a close-knit family ... "* –Variety. [5M, 5W] ISBN: 0-8222-1602-7

• **PSYCHOPATHIA SEXUALIS by John Patrick Shanley.** Fetishes and psychiatry abound in this scathing comedy about a man and his father's argyle socks. *"John Patrick Shanley's new play, PSYCHOPATHIA SEXUALIS is ... perfectly poised between daffy comedy and believable human neurosis which Shanley combines so well ... "* –The LA Times. *"John Patrick Shanley's PSYCHOPATHIA SEXUALIS is a salty boulevard comedy with a bittersweet theme ... "* –New York Magazine. *"A tour de force of witty, barbed dialogue."* –Variety. [3M, 2W] ISBN: 0-8222-1615-9

DRAMATISTS PLAY SERVICE, INC.
440 Park Avenue South, New York, NY 10016 212-683-8960 Fax 212-213-1539
postmaster@dramatists.com www.dramatists.com

NEW PLAYS

- **A QUESTION OF MERCY by David Rabe.** The Obie Award-winning playwright probes the sensitive and controversial issue of doctor-assisted suicide in the age of AIDS in this poignant drama. *"There are many devastating ironies in Mr. Rabe's beautifully considered, piercingly clear-eyed work ... " —The NY Times. "With unsettling candor and disturbing insight, the play arouses pity and understanding of a troubling subject ... Rabe's provocative tale is an affirmation of dignity that rings clear and true." —Variety.* [6M, 1W] ISBN: 0-8222-1643-4

- **A DOLL'S HOUSE by Henrik Ibsen, adapted by Frank McGuinness. Winner of the 1997 Tony Award for best revival.** *"New, raw, gut-twisting and gripping. Easily the hottest drama this season." —USA Today. "Bold, brilliant and alive." —The Wall Street Journal. "A thunderclap of an evening that takes your breath away." —Time. "The stuff of Broadway legend." —Associated Press.* [4M, 4W, 2 boys] ISBN: 0-8222-1636-1

- **THE WAITING ROOM by Lisa Loomer.** Three women from different centuries meet in a doctor's waiting room in this dark comedy about the timeless quest for beauty -- and its cost. *" ... THE WAITING ROOM ... is a bold, risky melange of conflicting elements that is ... terrifically moving ... There's no resisting the fierce emotional pull of the play." — The NY Times. " ... one of the high points of this year's Off-Broadway season ... THE WAITING ROOM is well worth a visit." —Back Stage.* [7M, 4W, flexible casting] ISBN: 0-8222-1594-2

- **MR. PETERS' CONNECTIONS by Arthur Miller.** Mr. Miller describes the protagonist as existing in a dream-like state when the mind is "freed to roam from real memories to conjectures, from trivialities to tragic insights, from terror of death to glorying in one's being alive." With this memory play, the Tony Award and Pulitzer Prize-winner reaffirms his stature as the world's foremost dramatist. *" ... a cross between Joycean stream-of-consciousness and Strindberg's dream plays, sweetened with a dose of William Saroyan's philosophical whimsy ... CONNECTIONS is most intriguing ... Miller scholars will surely find many connections of their own to make between this work and the author's earlier plays." —The NY Times.* [5M, 3W] ISBN: 0-8222-1687-6

- **THE STEWARD OF CHRISTENDOM by Sebastian Barry.** A freely imagined portrait of the author's great-grandfather, the last Chief Superintendent of the Dublin Metropolitan Police. *"MAGNIFICENT ... the cool, elegiac eye of James Joyce's THE DEAD; the bleak absurdity of Samuel Beckett's lost, primal characters; the cosmic anger of KING LEAR ... " —The NY Times. "Sebastian Barry's compassionate imaging of an ancestor he never knew is among the most poignant onstage displays of humanity in recent memory." —Variety.* [5M, 4W] ISBN: 0-8222-1609-4

- **SYMPATHETIC MAGIC by Lanford Wilson. Winner of the 1997 Obie for best play.** The mysteries of the universe, and of human and artistic creation, are explored in this award-winning play. *"Lanford Wilson's idiosyncratic SYMPATHETIC MAGIC is his BEST PLAY YET ... the rare play you WANT ... chock-full of ideas, incidents, witty or poetic lines, scientific and philosophical argument ... you'll find your intellectual faculties racing." — New York Magazine. "The script is like a fully notated score, next to which most new plays are cursory lead sheets." —The Village Voice.* [5M, 3W] ISBN: 0-8222-1630-2

DRAMATISTS PLAY SERVICE, INC.
440 Park Avenue South, New York, NY 10016 212-683-8960 Fax 212-213-1539
postmaster@dramatists.com www.dramatists.com